The short play remains popular today because it offers an interesting challenge to the writer, and a brief, intense experience to the audience or reader. In the space of a half-hour or so the dramatist must involve his two or three characters in a problem that will stimulate his audience to laughter, to suspense, or to serious thought as the action moves toward dramatic climax.

Some of the plays in this collection have achieved inter-national recognition. They all lend themselves to being read aloud with a separate reader for each part. But if you are reading privately, you can make a stage of your mind and on that stage direct a company of actors that you alone will see and hear. Charles Lamb, a writer in the early nineteenth century, said that sometimes the mind was the best place to stage a play, anyway.

—from the Introduction

JOHN STEVENS, editor of this collection of short plays, is the author of several books used in Canadian schools and colleges. He is also general editor of a series of acting edi-tions of Shakespearean plays produced in collaboration with stage directors at the Stratford Festival Theatre in Strat-ford, Canada. A professor of English at the Faculty of Education, University of Toronto, he has published many articles on literature and education.

Ten Canadian Short Plays

Edited by
John Stevens

A Dell Book

Published by
DELL DISTRIBUTING
A Division of Doubleday Canada Limited
105 Bond Street
Toronto, Ontario
M5B 1Y3

ISBN 0-440-95754-0

Printed and bound in Canada by Gagne Printing
Cover design by David Shaw
Reprinted by arrangement with Laurel Leaf Library, Dell Publishing Co. Inc.

ACKNOWLEDGMENTS

CONTENTS

INTRODUCTION

The short play remains popular today because it offers an interesting challenge to the writer, and a brief, intense experience to the audience or reader. In the space of a half-hour or so the dramatist must involve his two or three characters in a problem that will stimulate his audience to laughter, to suspense, or to serious thought as the action moves toward dramatic climax.

In some plays these elements of laughter, suspense and thought are held in balance, as in Norman Williams' play about teen-age rebellion, *Protest*. But in many plays one element predominates. In George Ryga's *Indian* and Gwen Ringwood's *Lament for Harmonica* the predominant element is thought. Both writers confront their audience with disturbing examples of the plight of North America's Indians and obviously want this plight to be considered seriously. In *The Raft* Stephen Leacock invites us to laugh at his shipwrecked couple and attaches no intellectual strings to the laughter. In *Flight into Danger* Arthur Hailey concentrates on his particular specialty—developing suspense. Probably no other TV suspense drama in the English language has been so popular a success as this classic about the hazards of air travel.

Some of the plays in this collection have achieved international recognition. Most of them have been prize-winners in Canada, and all of them, I hope, will interest you. They all lend themselves to being read aloud with a separate reader for each part. But if you are reading privately, you can make a stage of your mind and on that stage direct a company of actors that you alone will see and hear. Charles Lamb, a writer in the early nineteenth century, said that sometimes the mind was the best place to stage a play, anyway.

If you would like to find out more about the dramatists, further information is included at the end of this book.

—JOHN STEVENS

The Raft:
An Interlude

STEPHEN LEACOCK

(The kind of interlude that is sandwiched in for fifteen minutes between the dances in a musical revue.[1])

The curtain rises and the light comes on the stage slowly, gradually revealing a raft in the middle of the sea. The dawn is breaking. The raft has the stub of a mast sticking up on it and there is a chair on it and a litter of boxes and things.

On the raft is a man. He has on white flannel trousers, and a sky-blue flannel shirt, but no collar and tie.

He stands up and looks all around the horizon, his hand shading his eyes. He speaks in a sepulchral voice.

"Lost! Lost! Alone on the Caribbean Sea." [*In a more commonplace voice.*] "at least I think it's the Caribbean. It looks Caribbean to me. Lost! And not a woman in sight . . . I thought that in this kind of thing there is always a woman. Ha! Wait! There's one!"

> [*He is much excited and gets a long spy-glass and shoots it in and out at different lengths, searching the sea.*]

"No!—it's only seaweed . . . Ba!"

> [*He goes and sits down on a chair and yawns.*]

[1] It is to be noticed that this piece is all ready to put on the stage. Actors anxious for dramatic rights may apply by telegraph or on foot.

"I call this kind of thing dull! There's really nothing to do."

[*He gets a box of shoe polish and starts to polish his shoes with a rag. Presently—*]

"I think I'll look around for a woman again. It really is the only thing to do, on a raft—or anywhere else."

[*He takes his spy-glass and looks again.*]

"By Jove! Yes! yes! There's one floating in the sea right there. Quick! Quick!"

[*In great excitement he runs over to the mast, where a little looking-glass hangs, and starts putting on a collar and tie, and brushing his hair in terrible haste . . . He can't find his collar-stud, etc., etc., and keeps muttering—*]

"I must keep calm—a woman's life depends on my getting this collar on."

[*He looks over his shoulder.*]

"She's floating nearer—"

[*In the light of the rising sun the girl is now seen floating nearer and nearer.*]

"—and nearer—and she's a peach . . . I *must* save her! I must plunge in after her."

[*He stands in the attitude of a person about to dive into the sea, swinging his arms and counting.*]

"One—two—three—" [*nearly dives but checks himself and goes on*] "four—five—SIX . . . Ah, I forgot! I've no swimming costume . . . Wait a bit, though!"

[*He picks up off the raft a long, long pole with a hook on the end.*]

"Ha!"

[*The girl is quite near now. He hooks her on the pole and hauls her on to the raft . . . She sinks down flat on it, inanimate, her eyes closed, her face to the audience. Note: the girl of course is not wet: that would only mess the act up.*]

"What next? Ah, one moment."

[*He runs over to a little bookshelf that is stuck up on the top of the mast, takes out a book, sits down in a chair, and reads aloud very deliberately.*]

" 'Rules for re—for, re-sus—for resuscitating the

Damned—the Drowned: In resuscitating the drowned it must be remembered that not a moment must be lost.' "

[*He settles himself more comfortably in his chair to get a better light to read by.*]

" 'Every minute is of vital—of vital'—humph, I must get my eye glass."

[*He goes and hunts it up, polishes it and continues—*]

" 'Of vital importance. First, it is necessary to ascertain whether the heart is still beating.'—Ah!"

[*He gets off his chair and on to the floor of the raft on his toes and hands, makes the motions of attempting to put his ear close down on the girl's heart, but keeps withdrawing it with sudden shyness.*]

"Stop a bit."

[*He goes and gets a cardboard box and takes out a stethoscope so long that, still standing up, he fixes it to his ears and it reaches the girl's body. He listens and counts, his head on one side and with an air of great absorption.*]

"One."

[*A long pause.*]

"One and a half."

[*Another pause.*]

"One—eighty-five—right! She's alive!"

[*He gets his book again and reads.*]

" 'The strength of the circulation being different in the male and the female sex, the first thing to do if the victim is a woman is to rub her—to rub her—' "

[*He finds it difficult to read, and says conclusively—*]

"The first thing to do is to rubber. Oh, yes I see: Now where shall I begin? I'll rub her hands."

[*He takes one of her hands and strokes it very slowly in long loving strokes. After a moment he plucks at the lace cuff at her wrist.*]

"Ah, a laundry mark! her name! I must read. Her life hangs on it. 'Edith Croydon!' What a beautiful name!"

[*He goes on stroking her hand.*]

"It doesn't seem to revive her. Oh, very well, there's nothing for it."

[*He stands up with an air of great determination, and rolls back his cuffs.*]

"I must rub her legs."

[*The girl starts up.*]

"Don't you dare! You're no gentleman!"

"Miss Croydon, you misunderstand my motives!"

[*He walks away in a huff to the extreme end of the raft and stands with his back turned. The girl meantime runs to the mirror and starts doing her hair, etc.*]

"And for the matter of that, I *am* a gentleman. You'll find my card hanging there beside the mirror."

[*The girl picks down a large card that hangs beside the mirror and reads aloud.*]

" 'Harold Borus, Story Tale Adventurer, Rafts, Rescues and Other Specialities, Hairbreadth Escapes Shaved to Order.' Oh, Mr. Borus, I'm so sorry! Of course I know all about you—everybody does! I must apologize. Do come back on this part of the raft. Forgive me."

[BORUS, *coming back, and taking her hand with emotion.*]

"Miss Croydon, there is nothing to forgive! If I have saved your life, forget it. Let us never speak of it. Think of me not as a hero, but only as a man!"

"I will!"

"And meantime, please make yourself comfortable. Do take this chair. The entire raft, I need hardly say, is at your disposition. You'll find the view from the east side most interesting."

"Thank you so much."

[*They make themselves comfortable and intimate, she on the chair, he on the soap-box, with elaborate gestures of politeness.*]

"And do tell me, Mr. Borus, how did you get here?"

"Very gladly. You won't mind if I begin at the beginning?"

"Must you?"

"It's usual . . ."

"Oh, all right."

"Well then—" [*striking an attitude of recitation*] "Little did I think—"

"No, I suppose not."

"—when I left Havana in a packet—"

"Oh, Mr. Borus, who put you in a packet?"

"—in a packet-boat, that I should be wrecked on the dry Tortugas."

[THE GIRL, *clasping her hands with agitation.*]

"The *Dry* Tortugas! Oh, Mr. Borus, have the Tortugas gone dry?"

"We had hardly left when a great storm arose . . . A monstrous wave carried away the bridge."

"Good heavens!"

"We struggled on. A second wave carried away the rudder, the propeller, the wireless apparatus and the stethoscope!"

"Great heavens!"

"We struggled on. A third wave carried away the bar. It was at once decided to abandon the ship and lower the boats."

[THE GIRL, *perplexed.*]

"But why?"

"To look for the bar . . . In the confusion I was left behind. The storm subsided. I continued to make a raft out of a few loose iron beams fastened together by nuts."

"Fastened by nuts, Mr. Borus, but I thought you were the only one left in the ship?"

"—by nuts. This raft, Miss Croydon, cannot sink, it is all made of iron."

"How splendid! And now let me tell you my adventures."

"No, no, don't trouble, please. You're exhausted! Don't—you might faint!"

"Looking back" [THE GIRL *goes on very dramatically*] "it all seems a blank."

[BORUS *very hurriedly.*]

"All right, it's a blank. It's a blank. Let it go at that."

"Mr. Borus, I think you're terribly rude. You might let *me* tell *my* adventures!"

"Miss Croydon" [*very seriously*] "how many heroes are there in any story of adventure?"

"Only one."

"Well, I'm *it*. You must be something else."

[MISS CROYDON *pettishly*.]

"I don't want to be. All I know is that I'm cold and I'm hungry, and I don't think that I'll stay!"

"Cold! Hungry!"

[*He gets up and starts running round with animation, making preparations.*]

"Cold! Ha! ha! I'll soon have a fire for you!"

"A fire, Mr. Borus, how can you possibly start a fire?"

[BORUS *laughs*.]

"A very simple matter, Miss Croydon, to a trained hero like myself."

[*He has picked up an empty pan and set it on a box.*]

"I do it simply with sticks rubbed together."

"By rubbing dry sticks together! Like the Indians I've read about? How wonderful you are."

"I am."

[*He picks up two or three very little dry twigs.*]

"I take the dry sticks, so—"

"Yes! Yes!"

"And first rub them together, *so*—"

"Yes! Yes!"

"With a sort of twisting motion."

"Yes! Yes!"

"Then I put them in the pan with a bit of paper, *so*—" [*he takes out a match-box as he speaks*] "and strike a match and light them."

[*He lights the paper and the twigs and they blaze up in a little flame.* EDITH CROYDON *and* BORUS *warm their hands at it; she speaks.*]

"How really wonderful!"

"Yes. It's the Peruvian method! And now for food and drink."

[*The little fire presently flickers out, and has nothing more to do with the act.*]

"Have you food and drink on the raft, Mr. Borus? I think you are simply superb."

"I am. Now let me see." [*He starts taking things out of a box.*] "What have we here? Tinned pâté de foie gras."

"Lovely!"

"Canned asparagus. Do you like canned asparagus?"

"Oh, I worship it."

"Tin of boneless pheasant."

"Oh, Mr. Borus, I'm just mad over boneless pheasant!"

[BORUS, *taking out the cans and reading the labels, with exclamations from* THE GIRL—]

"Boneless pheasant—finless fish—spineless sardines —tongueless tongue—now what shall it be first?"

[BORUS *with great empressement has just laid a little white cloth on a soap-box, and quickly spread out glasses and dishes and knives and forks till it has the appearance of an appetizing preparation. They both accompany it with exclaimations of interest and delight.* MISS CROYDON *says*]

"Let me see. I think I'd like first, pâté de foie gras and finless fish, and just a teeny bit of shell-less lobster— and—and—"

[*When suddenly* BORUS *has sprung to his feet with a sort of howl.*]

"Oh, Mr. Borus, what is it?"

[BORUS, *casting his hands to heaven*—]

"I haven't got—I haven't got—"

"Yes—yes—"

"I forgot—"

"Yes—yes—you forgot—"

"The can opener! Great heavens, we have no can opener!"

[THE GIRL *exclaims*—] "No can opener!" [*and falls forward on the table.*]

BORUS: "Stop! Wake up! I can open them!"

[*He makes a wild attack on the tins, beating them, and stamping on them, and biting them, etc., etc. Presently he subsides in despair and collapses on the soap-box.*]

"It's no good, Miss Croydon. We must eat the tins. You eat first. You are a woman."

"No, Mr. Borus, not yet. We can at least" [*she speaks with tragedy*] "we can at least drink. Let us drink before we die."

"You are right. We can drink before we die. It is more than a lot of people can do."

[*He recovers something of his animation and begins taking out bottles and setting them on the table.*]

"There! Bottled ale. Bass's bottled ale!"

"Oh, Mr. Borus, how divine! I just worship Bass's bottled ale."

"Now then, get your glass ready."

"Right."

[*Then he leaps up again with a howl.*]

"What is it, Mr. Borus— Oh, what is it?"

"The thing—the thing you open it with! I haven't got one!"

[*They both collapse,* BORUS *slightly recovering, but gloomily*]:

"There's a way of opening these bottles with a fifty-cent piece . . ." [*feeling in his pocket*] "but I haven't got a fifty-cent piece."

[MISS CROYDON, *brightly*]

"Oh, never mind, I think I have a dollar bill in my purse."

[*Business here of trying to open the bottle by holding a dollar bill over it. At last* BORUS *says*]:

"It's no good, Miss Croydon. We must resign ourselves to our fate. If we must die" [*he takes a noble attitude*] "you are a woman. Die first!"

[*There is a sadness and then* MISS CROYDON *says*]:

"Mr. Borus, it's getting dark."

[BORUS *looks up at the sky.*]

"Yes, the sun will soon set."

"Already, Mr. Borus?"

"Yes, Miss Croydon. Night comes quickly in the tropics. Look, the sun is setting."

[*The sun, seen as a round, red disk at the back of the stage, begins to set in jumps, about a yard at a time. When it has got near the bottom it takes a long whirl up again and then goes under. The stage is half dark.*]

BORUS: "It is night!"

"Night! Here on the raft? Oh, I mustn't stay."

"Miss Croydon, I intend to treat you with the chivalry of a hero. One moment."

[BORUS *takes an oar and sticks it up, and takes a big gray blanket and fastens it across the raft like a partition, so as to divide the raft in two.*]

"Miss Croydon" [*says* BORUS, *looking over the top of the blanket*] "that end of the raft is absolutely *yours.*"

"How chivalrous you are!"

"Not at all. I shall not intrude upon you in any way. Good-night."

"Good-night, Mr. Borus."

[*They each begin making preparations for sleep, one each side of the curtain.* BORUS *stands up and puts his head over again.*]

"You'll find a candle and matches near your bed."

"Oh, thank you, Mr. Borus, how noble you are."

"Not at all."

[*After another little interlude* BORUS *puts his head over the top again.*]

"I am now putting my head over this blanket for the last time. If there is anything you want, say so now. And remember if you want anything in the night do not hesitate to call me. I shall be here—at any moment. I promise it. Good-night."

"Good-night, Mr. Borus."

[*They settle down in the growing darkness for a few minutes as if falling asleep. Then all of a sudden a bright light, a searchlight; comes shining over the sea, full on the raft. They both start up.*]

"Oh, Mr. Borus, look, look, a light—a ship!!"

BORUS: "A light—a ship! They may have a corkscrew! We're saved. Look—it's a large yacht—a pleasure yacht."

[*There are voices heard.*]

"Raft, Ahoy!" [*and shouts.*]

MISS CROYDON: "A pleasure yacht! Oh, then I recognize it!"

"You recognize it?"

"It's the yacht I fell out of this morning."

"Fell out of—"

"Yes. You wouldn't let me tell you . . ."

[*There is a call across the water.*]

"Raft ahoy! Stand by! We're lowering a boat."

BORUS: "Saved! Saved! But there is just one thing I want to say before we go aboard . . . Miss Croydon—Edith—since I've been on this raft I've learned to love you as I never could have anywhere else. Edith, will you be my wife?"

[MISS CROYDON, *falling into his arms*]:

"Will I? Oh, Harold, that's what I fell out of the yacht for!"

[*Curtain.*]

Flight into Danger

ARTHUR HAILEY

ACT I

FADE IN: *the passenger lobby of Winnipeg Air Terminal at night. At the departure counter of Cross-Canada Air-*

lines a male passenger agent in uniform (FIRST AGENT) *is checking a manifest. He reaches for p.a. mike.*

FIRST AGENT: Flight 98, direct fleet-liner service to Vancouver, with connections for Victoria, Seattle and Honolulu, leaving immediately through gate four. No smoking. All aboard, please.

> [*During the announcement* GEORGE SPENCER *enters through the main lobby doorway. About 35, he is a senior factory salesman for a motor truck manufacturer.* SPENCER *pauses to look for the Cross-Canada counter, then hastens toward it, arriving as the announcement concludes.*]

SPENCER: Is there space on Flight 98 for Vancouver?

FIRST AGENT: Sorry, sir, that flight is full. Did you check with Reservations?

SPENCER: Didn't have time. I came straight out on the chance you might have a "no show" seat.

FIRST AGENT: With the big football game on tomorrow in Vancouver, I don't think you'll have much chance of getting out before tomorrow afternoon.

SPENCER: That's no good. I've got to be in Vancouver tomorrow by midday.

FIRST AGENT [*hesitates*]: Look, I'm not supposed to tell you this, but there's a charter flight in from Toronto. They're going out to the coast for the game. I did hear they were a few seats light.

SPENCER: Who's in charge? Where do I find him?

FIRST AGENT: Ask at the desk over there. They call themselves Maple Leaf Air Charter. But mind, *I* didn't send you.

SPENCER [*smiles*]: Okay, thanks.

> [SPENCER *crosses to another departure counter which has a cardboard sign hanging behind it— Maple Leaf Air Charter. Behind the desk is an agent in a lounge suit. He is checking a manifest.*]

SPENCER: Excuse me.

SECOND AGENT: Yes?

SPENCER: I was told you might have space on a flight to Vancouver.

SECOND AGENT: Yes, there's one seat left. The flight's leaving right away though.

SPENCER: That's what I want.

SECOND AGENT: Very well, sir. Your name, please?

SPENCER: Spencer—George Spencer.

SECOND AGENT: That'll be fifty-five dollars for the one-way trip.

SPENCER: Will you take my air-travel card?

SECOND AGENT: No sir. Just old-fashioned cash.

SPENCER: All right.

[*Produces wallet and counts out bills.*]

SECOND AGENT [*handing over ticket*]: Do you have any bags?

SPENCER: One. Right here.

SECOND AGENT: All the baggage is aboard. Would you mind keeping that with you?

SPENCER: Be glad to.

SECOND AGENT: Okay, Mr. Spencer. Your ticket is your boarding pass. Go through gate three and ask the commissionaire for Flight 714. Better hurry.

SPENCER: Thanks a lot. Good night.

SECOND AGENT: Good night.

[*Exit* SPENCER. *Enter* STEWARDESS.]

SECOND AGENT: Hi, Janet. Did the meals get aboard?

STEWARDESS: Yes, they've just put them on. What was the trouble?

SECOND AGENT: Couldn't get service from the regular caterers here. We had to go to some outfit the other side of town. That's what held us up.

STEWARDESS: Are we all clear now?

SECOND AGENT: Yes, here's everything you'll need. [*Hands over papers.*] There's one more passenger. He's just gone aboard. So that's 56 souls in your lovely little hands.

STEWARDESS: I'll try not to drop any.

SECOND AGENT [*reaching for coat*]: Well, I'm off home.

STEWARDESS [*as she leaves*]: 'Night.

SECOND AGENT [*pulling on coat*]: 'Night, Janet.

[*Calls after her.*] Don't forget to cheer for the Blue Bombers tomorrow.

[STEWARDESS *waves and smiles.*]

[DISSOLVE TO: *the passenger cabin of a DC-4 liner. There is one empty aisle seat. Seated next to it is* DR. FRANK BAIRD, M.D., 55. GEORGE SPENCER *enters, sees the unoccupied seat and comes toward it.*]

SPENCER: Pardon me, is this anyone's seat?

BAIRD: No.

SPENCER: Thanks.

[SPENCER *sheds his topcoat and puts it on the rack above the seats. Meanwhile the plane's motors can be heard starting.*

[CUT TO: FILM INSERT—*four-engined airplane exterior, night: the motors starting.*

[CUT TO: *the passenger cabin.*]

BAIRD: I presume you're going to the big game like the rest of us.

SPENCER: I'm ashamed to admit it, but I'd forgotten about the game.

BAIRD: I wouldn't say that too loudly if I were you. Some of the more exuberant fans might tear you limb from limb.

SPENCER: I'll keep my voice down. [*Pleasantly.*] Matter of fact, I'm making a sales trip to the coast.

BAIRD: What do you sell?

SPENCER: Trucks.

BAIRD: Trucks?

SPENCER: That's right. I'm what the local salesmen call the son-of-a-gun from head office with the special prices. Need any trucks? How about forty? Give you a real good discount today.

BAIRD [*laughs*]: I couldn't use that many, I'm afraid. Not in my line.

SPENCER: Which is?

BAIRD: Medicine.

SPENCER: You mean you're a doctor?

BAIRD: That's right. Can't buy one truck, leave alone

forty. Football is the one extravagance I allow myself.

SPENCER: Delighted to hear it, Doctor. Now I can relax.

[*As he speaks, the run-up of the aircraft engines begins, increasing to a heavy roar.*]

BAIRD [*raising his voice*]: Do you think you can in this racket? I never can figure out why they make all this noise before take-off.

SPENCER [*shouting, as noise increases*]: It's the normal run-up of the engines. Airplane engines don't use battery ignition like you have in your car. They run on magneto ignition, and each of the magnetos is tested separately. If they're okay and the motors are giving all the power they should—away you go!

BAIRD: You sound as if you know something about it.

SPENCER: I'm pretty rusty now. I used to fly fighters in the air force. But that was ten years ago. Reckon I've forgotten most of it. Well, there we go.

[*The tempo of the motors increases.* BAIRD *and* SPENCER *lean toward the window to watch the take-off, although it is dark outside.*

[CUT TO: *the passenger cabin. The noise of the motor is reduced slightly and the two men relax in their seats.* SPENCER *reaches for cigarettes.*]

SPENCER: Smoke?

BAIRD: Thank you.

[*They light up.* STEWARDESS *enters from aft of airplane and reaches for two pillows from the rack above.*]

STEWARDESS: We were held up at Winnipeg, sir, and we haven't served dinner yet. Would you care for some?

SPENCER: Yes, please.

[STEWARDESS *puts a pillow on his lap.*]

STEWARDESS [*to* BAIRD]: And you, sir?

BAIRD: Thank you, yes. [*To* SPENCER.] It's a bit late for dinner, but it'll pass the time away.

STEWARDESS: There's lamb chops or grilled halibut.

BAIRD: I'll take the lamb.

SPENCER: Yes, I'll have that, too.

STEWARDESS: Thank you, sir.

BAIRD [*to* SPENCER]: Tell me . . . By the way, my name is Baird.

SPENCER: Spencer. George Spencer.

[*They shake hands.*]

BAIRD: How'd'do. Tell me, when you make a sales trip like this do you . . .

[*Fade voices and pan with the* STEWARDESS *returning aft. Entering the airplane's tiny galley she picks up a telephone and presses a call button.*]

VOICE OF FIRST OFFICER: Flight deck.

STEWARDESS: I'm finally serving the dinners. What'll "you-all" have—lamb chops or grilled halibut?

VOICE OF THE FIRST OFFICER: Just a minute. [*Pause.*] Skipper says he'll have the lamb . . . Oh, hold it! . . . No, he's changed his mind. Says he'll take the halibut. Make it two fish, Janet.

STEWARDESS: Okay.

[STEWARDESS *hangs up the phone and begins to arrange meal trays.*

[CUT TO: SPENCER *and* BAIRD.]

SPENCER: No, I hadn't expected to go west again this quickly.

BAIRD: You have my sympathy. I prescribe my travel in small doses. [STEWARDESS *enters and puts meal tray on pillow.*] Oh, thank you.

STEWARDESS: Will you have coffee, tea or milk, sir?

BAIRD: Coffee, please.

STEWARDESS: I'll bring it later.

BAIRD: That'll be fine. [To SPENCER.] Tell me, do you follow football at all?

SPENCER: A little. Hockey's my game, though. Who are you for tomorrow?

BAIRD: The Argos, naturally. [*As the* STEWARDESS *brings second tray.*] Thank you, dear.

STEWARDESS: Will you have coffee, tea or . . .

SPENCER: I'll have coffee too. No cream. [STEWARDESS *nods and exits. To* BAIRD.] Must be a calm night outside. No trouble in keeping the dinner steady.

BAIRD [*looking out of window*]: It *is* calm. Not a

cloud in sight. Must be a monotonous business flying these things once they're off the ground.

SPENCER: It varies, I guess.

[AUDIO: *fades up the roar of motors.*

[DISSOLVE TO: FILM INSERT—*airplane in level flight, night.*

[DISSOLVE TO: *the aircraft flight deck. The* CAPTAIN *is seated on left,* FIRST OFFICER *on right. Neither is touching the controls.*]

FIRST OFFICER [*into radio mike*]: Height 16,000 feet. Course 285 true. ETA Vancouver 0505 Pacific Standard. Over.

RADIO VOICE: Flight 714. This is Winnipeg Control. Roger. Out.

[*The* FIRST OFFICER *reaches for a log sheet and makes a notation, then relaxes in his seat.*]

FIRST OFFICER: Got any plans for Vancouver?

CAPTAIN: Yes, I'm going to sleep for two whole days.

[*The* STEWARDESS *enters with a meal tray.*]

STEWARDESS: Who's first?

CAPTAIN: You take yours, Harry.

[STEWARDESS *produces a pillow and the* FIRST OFFICER *slides back his seat, well clear of control column. He places the pillow on his knees and accepts the tray.*]

FIRST OFFICER: Thanks, honey.

CAPTAIN: Everything all right at the back, Janet? How are the football fans?

STEWARDESS: They tired themselves out on the way from Toronto. Looks like a peaceful, placid night.

FIRST OFFICER [*with mouth full of food, raising fork for emphasis*]: Aha! Those are the sort of nights to beware of. It's in the quiet times that trouble brews. I'll bet you right now that somebody's getting ready to be sick.

STEWARDESS: That'll be when you're doing the flying. Or have you finally learned how to hold this thing steady? [*To* CAPTAIN.] How's the weather?

CAPTAIN: General fog east of the mountains, extending pretty well as far as Manitoba. But it's clear to the west. Should be rockaby smooth the whole way.

STEWARDESS: Good. Well, keep Junior here off the controls while I serve coffee. [*Exits.*]

FIRST OFFICER [*calling after her*]: Mark my words, woman! Stay close to that mop and pail.

CAPTAIN: How's the fish?

FIRST OFFICER [*hungrily*]: Not bad. Not bad at all. If there were about three times as much it might be a square meal.

[AUDIO: *fade voices into roar of motors.*

[DISSOLVE TO: *the passenger cabin.* SPENCER *and* BAIRD *are concluding their meal.* BAIRD *puts down a coffee cup and wipes his mouth with a napkin. Then he reaches up and presses a call button over his head. There is a soft "ping" and the* STEWARD-ESS *enters.*]

STEWARDESS: Yes, sir?

BAIRD: That was very enjoyable. Now if you'll take the tray I think I'll try to sleep.

STEWARDESS: Surely. [*To* SPENCER.] Will you have more coffee, sir?

SPENCER: No thanks. [STEWARDESS *picks up the second tray and goes aft.* SPENCER *yawns.*] Let me know if the noise keeps you awake. If it does, I'll have the engines stopped.

BAIRD [*chuckles*]: Well, at least there won't be any night calls—I hope.

[BAIRD *reaches up and switches off the overhead reading lights so that both seats are in semi-darkness. The two men prepare to sleep.*

[DISSOLVE TO: FILM INSERT—*airplane in level flight, night.*

[DISSOLVE TO: *the passenger cabin. The* CAPTAIN *emerges from the flight deck and strolls aft, saying "Good evening" to one or two people who glance up as he goes by. He passes* SPENCER *and* BAIRD, *who are sleeping. As the* CAPTAIN *progresses, the* STEWARDESS *can be seen at the rear of the cabin. She is bending solicitously over a woman passenger, her hand on the woman's forehead. The* CAPTAIN *approaches.*]

CAPTAIN: Something wrong, Miss Burns?

STEWARDESS: This lady is feeling a little unwell. I was going to get her some aspirin. [*To the woman passenger*.] I'll be back in a moment.

CAPTAIN: Sorry to hear that. What seems to be the trouble?

[*The* WOMAN PASSENGER *has her head back and her mouth open. A strand of hair has fallen across her face and she is obviously in pain.*]

FIRST WOMAN PASSENGER [*speaking with effort*]: I'm sorry to be such a nuisance. but it hit me all of a sudden . . . just a few minutes ago . . . dizziness and nausea and a sharp pain . . . [*indicating abdomen*] down here.

CAPTAIN: Well, I think the stewardess will be able to help you.

[STEWARDESS *returns.*]

STEWARDESS: Now. here you are; try these.

[*She hands over two aspirins and a cup of water. The* PASSENGER *takes them, then puts her head back on the seat rest.*]

FIRST WOMAN PASSENGER: Thank you very much.

[*She smiles faintly at the* CAPTAIN.]

CAPTAIN [*quietly, taking* STEWARDESS *aside*]: If she gets any worse you'd better let me know and I'll radio ahead. But we've still five hours' flying to the coast. Is there a doctor on board, do you know?

STEWARDESS: There was no one listed as a doctor on the manifest. But I can go around and ask.

CAPTAIN [*looks around*]: Well, most everybody's sleeping now. We'd better not disturb them unless we have to. See how she is in the next half-hour or so. [CAPTAIN *bends down and puts a hand on the* WOMAN'S *shoulder.*] Try to rest, madam, if you can. Miss Burns will take good care of you.

[*The* CAPTAIN *nods to* STEWARDESS *and begins his return to the flight deck. The* STEWARDESS *arranges blanket around the* WOMAN PASSENGER. SPENCER *and* BAIRD *are still sleeping as the* CAPTAIN *passes.*

[DISSOLVE TO: FILM INSERT—*airplane in level flight, night.*

[DISSOLVE TO: *the passenger cabin.* SPENCER *stirs and wakes. Then he glances forward to where the* STEWARDESS *is leaning over another section of seats and her voice can be heard softly.*]

STEWARDESS: I'm sorry to disturb you, but we're trying to find out if there's a doctor on board.

FIRST MALE PASSENGER: Not me, I'm afraid. Is something wrong?

STEWARDESS: One of the passengers is feeling unwell. It's nothing too serious. [*Moving on to the next pair of seats.*] I'm sorry to disturb you, but we're trying to find out if there's a doctor on board.

[*There is an indistinct answer from the two people just questioned, then* SPENCER *sits forward and calls the* STEWARDESS.]

SPENCER: Stewardess! [*Indicating* BAIRD, *who is still sleeping.*] This gentleman is a doctor.

STEWARDESS: Thank you. I think we'd better wake him. I have two passengers who are quite sick.

SPENCER: All right. [*Shaking* BAIRD'S *arm.*] Doctor! Doctor! Wake up!

BAIRD: Um. Um. What is it?

STEWARDESS: Doctor, I'm sorry to disturb you. But we have two passengers who seem quite sick. I wonder if you'd take a look at them.

BAIRD [*sleepily*]: Yes . . . yes . . . of course.

[SPENCER *moves out of seat to permit* BAIRD *to reach the aisle.* BAIRD *then follows the* STEWARDESS *aft to the* FIRST WOMAN PASSENGER. *Although a blanket is around her, the woman is shivering and gasping, with her head back and eyes closed. The* DOCTOR *places a hand on her forehead and she opens her eyes.*]

STEWARDESS: This gentleman is a doctor. He's going to help us.

FIRST WOMAN PASSENGER: Oh, Doctor . . . !

BAIRD: Now just relax. [*He makes a quick external examination, first checking pulse, then taking a small pen-type flashlight from his pocket and looking into her eyes. He then loosens the blanket and the* WOMAN's *coat beneath the blanket. As he places a hand on her abdomen she gasps with pain.*] Hurt you there? [*With an effort she nods.*] There?

FIRST WOMAN PASSENGER: Oh yes! Yes!

[BAIRD *replaces the coat and blanket, then turns to* STEWARDESS.]

BAIRD [*with authority*]: Please tell the Captain we must land at once. This woman has to be gotten to hospital immediately.

STEWARDESS: Do you know what's wrong, Doctor?

BAIRD: I can't tell. I've no means of making a proper diagnosis. But it's serious enough to land at the nearest city with hospital facilities. You can tell your Captain that.

STEWARDESS: Very well, Doctor. [*Moving across the aisle and forward.*] While I'm gone will you take a look at this gentleman here? He's also complained of sickness and stomach pains.

[BAIRD *goes to a* MALE PASSENGER *indicated by the* STEWARDESS. *The man is sitting forward and resting his head on the back of the seat ahead of him. He is retching.*]

BAIRD: I'm a doctor. Will you put your head back, please? [*The man groans, but follows the doctor's instruction. He is obviously weak.* BAIRD *makes another quick examination, then pauses thoughtfully.*] What have you had to eat in the last twenty-four hours?

SECOND MALE PASSENGER [*with effort*]: Just the usual meals . . . breakfast . . . bacon and eggs . . . salad for lunch . . . couple of sandwiches at the airport . . . then dinner here.

[*The* STEWARDESS *enters, followed by the* CAPTAIN.]

BAIRD [*to* STEWARDESS]: Keep him warm. Get blankets around him. [*To* CAPTAIN.] How quickly can we land, Captain?

CAPTAIN: That's the trouble. I've just been talking to Calgary. There was light fog over the prairies earlier, but now it's thickened and everything is closed in this side of the mountains. It's clear at the coast and we'll have to go through.

BAIRD: Is that faster than turning back?

CAPTAIN: It would take us longer to go back now than to go on.

BAIRD: Then how soon do you expect to land?

CAPTAIN: At about five A.M. Pacific time. [*As* BAIRD *glances at his watch.*] You need to put your watch on two hours because of the change of time. We'll be landing in three hours forty-five minutes from now.

BAIRD: Then I'll have to do what I can for these people. Can my bag be reached? I checked it at Toronto.

CAPTAIN: We can get it. Let me have your tags, Doctor.

> [BAIRD *takes out a wallet and selects two baggage tags which he hands to* CAPTAIN.]

BAIRD: There are two bags. It's the small overnight case I want.

> [*As he finishes speaking the airplane lurches violently.* BAIRD *and the* STEWARDESS *and the* CAPTAIN *are thrown sharply to one side. Simultaneously the telephone in the galley buzzes several times. As the three recover their balance the* STEWARDESS *answers the phone quickly.*]

STEWARDESS: Yes?

FIRST OFFICER'S VOICE [*under strain*]: Come forward quickly. I'm sick!

STEWARDESS: The First Officer is sick. He says come quickly.

CAPTAIN [*to* BAIRD]: You'd better come too.

> [*The* CAPTAIN *and* BAIRD *move quickly forward, passing through the flight deck door.*
>
> [CUT TO: *the flight deck. The* FIRST OFFICER *is at the controls on the right-hand side. He is retching and shuddering, flying the airplane by will-power and nothing else. The* CAPTAIN *promptly slides into the left-hand seat and takes the controls.*]

CAPTAIN: Get him out of there!

> [*Together* BAIRD *and the* STEWARDESS *lift the* FIRST OFFICER *from his seat and, as they do, he*

collapses. They lower him to the floor and the STEWARDESS *reaches for a pillow and blankets.* BAIRD *makes the same quick examination he used in the two previous cases. Meanwhile the* CAPTAIN *has steadied the aircraft and now he snaps over a button to engage the automatic pilot. He releases the controls and turns to the others, though without leaving his seat.*]

CAPTAIN: He must have been changing course when it happened. We're back on auto pilot now. Now, Doctor, what is it? What's happening?

BAIRD: There's a common denominator in these attacks. There has to be. And the most likely thing is food. [*To* STEWARDESS.] How long is it since we had dinner?

STEWARDESS: Two and a half to three hours.

BAIRD: Now then, what did you serve?

STEWARDESS: Well, the main course was a choice of fish or meat.

BAIRD: I remember that. I ate meat. [*Indicating* FIRST OFFICER.] What did he have?

STEWARDESS [*faintly, with dawning alarm*]: Fish.

BAIRD: Do you remember what the other two passengers had?

STEWARDESS: No.

BAIRD: Then go back quickly and find out, please. [*As the* STEWARDESS *exits* BAIRD *kneels beside* FIRST OFFICER, *who is moaning.*] Try to relax. I'll give you something in a few minutes to help the pain. You'll feel better if you stay warm.

[BAIRD *arranges the blanket around the* FIRST OFFICER. *Now the* STEWARDESS *reappears.*]

STEWARDESS [*alarmed*]: Doctor, both those passengers had fish. And there are three more cases now. And they ate fish too. Can you come?

BAIRD: Yes, but I need that bag of mine.

CAPTAIN: Janet, take these tags and get one of the passengers to help you. [*Hands over* BAIRD'S *luggage tags.*] Doctor, I'm going to get on the radio and report what's happening to Vancouver. Is there anything you want to add?

BAIRD: Yes. Tell them we have three serious cases of suspected food poisoning and there appear to be others. When we land we'll want ambulances and medical help waiting, and the hospitals should be warned. Tell them we're not sure, but we suspect the poisoning may have been caused by fish served on board. You'd better suggest they put a ban on serving all food which originated wherever ours came from until we've established the source for sure.

CAPTAIN: Right. [*He reaches for the radio mike and* BAIRD *turns to go aft. But suddenly a thought strikes the* CAPTAIN.] Doctor, I've just remembered . . .

BAIRD: Yes.

CAPTAIN [*quietly*]: I ate fish.

BAIRD: When?

CAPTAIN: I'd say about half an hour after he did. [*Pointing to* FIRST OFFICER.] Maybe a little longer. Is there anything I can do?

BAIRD: It doesn't follow that everyone will be affected. There's often no logic to these things. You feel all right now?

CAPTAIN: Yes.

BAIRD: You'd better not take any chances. Your food can't be completely digested yet. As soon as I get my bag I'll give you something to help you get rid of it.

CAPTAIN: Then hurry, Doctor. For God's sake, hurry! [*Into mike.*] Vancouver Control. This is Maple Leaf Charter Flight 714. I have an emergency message. Do you read? Over.

VOICE ON RADIO [VANCOUVER OPERATOR]: Go ahead, 714.

CAPTAIN: We have serious food poisoning on board. Several passengers and the First Officer are seriously ill . . .

> [DISSOLVE TO: *the luggage compartment below the flight deck. A passenger is hurriedly passing up bags to the* STEWARDESS. BAIRD *is looking down from above.*]

BAIRD: That's it! That's it down there! Let me have it!

[FADE OUT]

ACT II

FADE IN: *the Control Room, Vancouver Airport. At a radio panel an* OPERATOR, *wearing headphones, is transcribing a message on a typewriter. Part way through the message he presses a button on the panel and a bell rings stridently, signalling an emergency. At once an* AIRPORT CONTROLLER *appears behind the* OPERATOR *and reads the message as it continues to come in. Nearby is a telephone switchboard manned by an operator, and a battery of teletypes clattering noisily.*

CONTROLLER [*over his shoulder, to* SWITCHBOARD OPERATOR]: Get me area traffic control, then clear the teletype circuit to Winnipeg. Priority message. [*Stepping back to take phone.*] Vancouver Controller here. I've an emergency report from Maple Leaf Charter Flight 714, ex-Winnipeg for Vancouver. There's serious food poisoning among the passengers and the First Officer is down too. They're asking for all levels below them to be cleared, and priority approach and landing. ETA is 0505 . . . Roger. We'll keep you posted. [*To a* TELETYPE OPERATOR, *who has appeared.*] Got Winnipeg? [*As* TELETYPE OPERATOR *nods.*] Send this message. Controller Winnipeg. Urgent. Maple Leaf Charter Flight 714 reports serious food poisoning among passengers believed due to fish dinner served on flight. Imperative check source and suspend all other food service originating same place. That's all. [*To* SWITCHBOARD OPERATOR.] Get me the local agent for Maple Leaf Charter. Burdick's his name—call his home. And after that I want the city police—the senior officer on duty. [CONTROLLER *crosses to radio control panel and reads message which is just being completed. To* RADIO OPERATOR.] Acknowledge. Say that all altitudes below

them are being cleared and they'll be advised of landing
instructions here. Ask them to keep us posted on condition of the passengers.

SWITCHBOARD OPERATOR: Mr. Burdick is here at the
airport. I have him on the line now.

CONTROLLER: Good. Controller here. Burdick, we've
got an emergency message on one of your flights—714,
ex-Toronto and Winnipeg. [*Pause.*] No, the aircraft is
all right. There's food poisoning among the passengers
and the First Officer has it too. You'd better come over.
[*Replaces phone. Then to* SWITCHBOARD OPERATOR.]
Have you got the police yet? [*As* OPERATOR *nods.*]
Right, put it on this line. Hullo, this is the Controller,
Vancouver Airport. Who am I speaking to, please?
[*Pause.*] Inspector, we have an emergency on an incoming flight. Several of the passengers are seriously ill
and we need ambulances and doctors out here at the airport. [*Pause.*] Six people for sure, maybe more. The
flight will be landing at five minutes past five local time
—that's in about three and a half hours. Now, will you
get the ambulances, set up traffic control and alert the
hospitals? Right. We'll call you again as soon as there's
anything definite.

> [*During the above,* HARRY BURDICK, *local manager
> of Maple Leaf Air Charter, has entered.*]

BURDICK: Where's the message?

> [RADIO OPERATOR *hands him a copy, which* BUR-
> DICK *reads.*]

BURDICK [*to* RADIO OPERATOR]: How's the weather
at Calgary? It might be quicker to go in there.

CONTROLLER: No dice! There's fog down to the
deck everywhere east of the Rockies. They'll have to
come through.

BURDICK: Let me see the last position report. [*As*
CONTROLLER *passes a clip board.*] You say you've got
medical help coming?

CONTROLLER: The city police are working on it now.

BURDICK: That message! They say the First Officer
is down. What about the Captain? Ask if he's affected,

and ask if there's a doctor on board. Tell them we're getting medical advice here in case they need it.

CONTROLLER: I'll take care of that.

BURDICK [*to* SWITCHBOARD OPERATOR]: Will you get me Doctor Knudsen, please. You'll find his home number on the emergency list.

CONTROLLER [*into radio mike*]: Flight 714, this is Vancouver.

[DISSOLVE TO: *the airplane passenger cabin.* BAIRD *is leaning over another prostrate passenger. The main lighting is on in the cabin and other passengers, so far not affected, are watching with varying degrees of concern and anxiety. Some have remained in their seats, others have clustered in the aisle. The* DOCTOR *has obtained his bag and it is open beside him. The* STEWARDESS *is attending to another passenger nearby.*]

BAIRD [*to* STEWARDESS]: I think I'd better talk to everyone and tell them the story. [*Moving to centre of cabin, he raises his voice.*] Ladies and gentlemen, may I have your attention, please? If you can't hear me, perhaps you would come a little closer. [*Pause, as passengers move in.*] My name is Baird and I am a doctor. I think it's time that everyone knew what is happening. So far as I can tell, we have several cases of food poisoning and we believe that the cause of it was the fish which was served for dinner.

SECOND WOMAN PASSENGER [*with alarm, to man beside her*]: Hector! We both had fish!

BAIRD: Now, there is no immediate cause for alarm or panic, and even if you did eat fish for dinner, it doesn't follow that you are going to be affected too. There's seldom any logic to these things. However, we *are* going to take some precautions and the stewardess and I are coming around to everyone, and I want you to tell us if you ate fish. If you did we'll tell you what to do to help yourselves. Now, if you'll go back to your seats we'll begin right away. [*To* STEWARDESS, *as passengers move back to their seats.*] All we can do now is to give immediate first aid.

STEWARDESS: What should that be, Doctor?

BAIRD: Two things. First, everyone who ate fish must drink several glasses of water. That will help to dilute the poison. After that we'll give an emetic. I have some emetic pills in my bag, and if there aren't enough we'll have to rely on salt. Do you have salt in the galley?

STEWARDESS: A few small packets which go with the lunches, but we can break them open.

BAIRD: All right. We'll see how far the pills will go first. I'll start at the back here. Meanwhile you begin giving drinking water to the passengers already affected and get some to the First Officer too. I'll ask someone to help you.

FIRST MALE PASSENGER: Can I help, Doctor?

BAIRD: What did you eat for dinner—fish or meat?

FIRST MALE PASSENGER: Meat.

BAIRD: All right. Will you help the stewardess bring glasses of water to the people who are sick? I want them to drink at least three glasses each—more if they can.

STEWARDESS [going to galley]: We'll use these cups. There's drinking water here and at the rear.

FIRST MALE PASSENGER: All right, let's get started.

BAIRD [to STEWARDESS]: The Captain! Before you do anything else you'd better get him on to drinking water, and give him two emetic pills. Here. [Takes bottle from his bag and shakes out the pills.] Tell him they'll make him feel sick, and the sooner he is, the better.

STEWARDESS: Very well, Doctor.

SECOND WOMAN PASSENGER [frightened]: Doctor! Doctor! I heard you say the pilots are ill. What will happen to us if they can't fly the plane? Hector, I'm frightened.

THIRD MALE PASSENGER: Take it easy, my dear. Nothing has happened so far and the doctor is doing all he can.

BAIRD: I don't think you'll have any reason to worry, madam. It's quite true that both of the pilots had the fish which we believe may have caused the trouble. But only the First Officer is affected. Now, did you and your husband eat fish or meat?

THIRD MALE PASSENGER: Fish. We both ate fish.

BAIRD: Then will you both drink at least—better make it four—of those cups of water which the other gentleman is bringing around. After that, take one of these pills each. [*Smiling.*] I think you'll find there are little containers under your seat. Use those. [*Goes to rear of plane.*]

FOURTH MALE PASSENGER [*in broad English Yorkshire accent*]: How's it comin', Doc? Everything under control?

BAIRD: I think we're holding our own. What did you have for dinner?

FOURTH MALE PASSENGER: Ah had the bloomin' fish. Didn't like it neither. Fine how-d'you-do this is. Coom all this way t'see our team win, and now it looks like Ah'm headed for a mortuary slab.

BAIRD: It really isn't as bad as that, you know. But just as a precaution, drink four cups of water—it's being brought around now—and after that take this pill. It'll make you feel sick.

FOURTH MALE PASSENGER [*pulling carton from under seat and holding it up*]: It's the last time I ride on a bloomin' airplane! What a service! They give you your dinner and then coom round and ask for it back.

BAIRD: What did you have for dinner, please—meat or fish?

SECOND MALE PASSENGER: Meat, Doctor.

FIFTH MALE PASSENGER: Yes, I had meat too.

BAIRD: All right, we won't worry about you.

SIXTH MALE PASSENGER: I had meat, Doctor.

SEVENTH MALE PASSENGER: I had fish.

BAIRD: Very well. Will you drink at least four cups of water, please? It'll be brought round to you. Then take this pill.

SIXTH MALE PASSENGER [*slow-speaking; a little dull-witted*]: What's caused this food poisoning, Doctor?

BAIRD: Well, it can either be caused through spoilage of the food, or some kind of bacteria—the medical word is staphylococcus poisoning.

SIXTH MALE PASSENGER [*nodding knowledgeably*]: Oh, yes . . . staphylo . . . I see.

BAIRD: Either that, or some toxic substance may have gotten into the food during its preparation.

SEVENTH MALE PASSENGER: Which kind do you think this is, Doctor?

BAIRD: From the effect I suspect a toxic substance.

SEVENTH MALE PASSENGER: And you don't know what it is?

BAIRD: We won't know until we make laboratory tests. Actually, with modern food-handling methods— the chances of this happening are probably a million to one against.

STEWARDESS [*entering*]: I couldn't get the First Officer to take more than a little water, Doctor. He seems pretty bad.

BAIRD: I'll go to him now. Have you checked all the passengers in the front portion?

STEWARDESS: Yes, and there are two more new cases —the same symptoms as the others.

BAIRD: I'll attend to them—after I've looked at the First Officer.

STEWARDESS: Do you think . . .

[*Before the sentence is completed the galley telephone buzzes insistently.* BAIRD *and the* STEWARDESS *exchange glances quickly, then, without waiting to answer the phone, race to the flight deck door.*

[CUT TO: *the flight deck. The* CAPTAIN *is in the left-hand seat. Sweat pouring down his face, he is racked by retching and his right hand is on his stomach. Yet he is fighting against the pain and attempting to reach the radio transmitter mike. But he doesn't make it and, as* BAIRD *and the* STEWARDESS *reach him, he falls back in his seat.*]

CAPTAIN [*weakly*]: I did what you said . . . guess it was too late . . . You've got to give me something, Doctor . . . so I can hold out . . . till I see this airplane on the ground . . . You understand? . . . It'll fly itself on this course . . . but I've got to take it in . . . Get on the radio . . . Tell control . . .

[*During the above* BAIRD *and the* STEWARDESS *have been helping the* CAPTAIN *from his seat. Now he collapses into unconsciousness and* BAIRD *goes down beside him. The* DOCTOR *has a stethoscope now and uses it, then makes the other checks quickly and efficiently.*]

BAIRD: Get blankets over him. Keep him warm. There's probably a reaction because he tried to fight it off so long.

STEWARDESS [*alarmed*]: Can you do what he said? Can you bring him round long enough to land?

BAIRD [*bluntly*]: You're part of this crew, so I'll tell you how things are. Unless I can get him to a hospital quickly I'm not even sure I can save his life. And that goes for the others too.

STEWARDESS: But . . .

BAIRD: I know what you're thinking, and I've thought of it too. How many passengers are there on board?

STEWARDESS: Fifty-six.

BAIRD: And how many fish dinners did you serve?

STEWARDESS [*composing herself*]: Probably about fifteen. More people ate meat than fish, and some didn't eat at all because it was so late.

BAIRD: And you?

STEWARDESS: I had meat.

BAIRD [*quietly*]: My dear, did you ever hear the term "long odds"?

STEWARDESS: Yes, but I'm not sure what it means.

BAIRD: I'll give you an example. Out of a total field of 55, our chance of safety depends on there being one person back there who not only is qualified to land this airplane, but who didn't choose fish for dinner tonight.

[*After her initial alarm the* STEWARDESS *is calm now, and competent. She looks* BAIRD *in the eye and even manages a slight smile.*]

STEWARDESS: Then I suppose I should begin asking.

BAIRD [*thoughtfully*]: Yes, but there's no sense in starting a panic. [*Decisively.*] You'd better do it this way. Say that the First Officer is sick and the Captain wondered if there's someone with flying experience who could help him with the radio.

STEWARDESS: Very well, Doctor. [*She turns to go.*]

BAIRD: Wait! The man who was sitting beside me! He said something about flying in the war. And we both ate meat. Get him first! But still go round the others. There may be someone else with more experience.

[STEWARDESS *exits and* BAIRD *busies himself with the* FIRST OFFICER *and the* CAPTAIN. *After a moment,* GEORGE SPENCER *enters.*]

SPENCER: The Stewardess said . . . [*Then, as he sees the two pilots.*] No! Not both pilots!

BAIRD: Can *you* fly this airplane—and land it?

SPENCER: No! No! Not a chance! Of course not!

BAIRD: But you told me you flew in the war.

SPENCER: So I did. But that was fighters—little combat airplanes, not a great ship like this. I flew airplanes which had one engine. This has four. Flying characteristics are different. Controls don't react the same way. It's another kind of flying altogether. And besides that, I haven't touched an airplane for over ten years.

BAIRD [*grimly*]: Then let's hope there's someone else on board who can do the job . . . because neither of these men can.

[STEWARDESS *enters and pauses.*]

STEWARDESS [*quietly*]: There's no one else.

BAIRD: Mr. Spencer, I know nothing of flying. I have no means of evaluating what you tell me. All I know is this: that among the people on this airplane who are physically able to fly it, you are the only one with any kind of qualifications to do so. What do you suggest?

SPENCER [*desperately*]: Isn't there a chance—of either pilot recovering?

BAIRD: I'll tell you what I just told the stewardess here. Unless I can get them to hospital quickly, I can't even be sure of saving their lives.

[*There is a pause.*]

SPENCER: Well—I guess I just got drafted. If either of you are any good at praying, you can start any time. [*He slips into the left-hand seat.*] Let's take a look. Altitude 16,000. Course 290. The ship's on automatic pilot—we can be thankful for that. Air speed 210 knots. [*Touching the various controls.*] Throttles, pitch, mixture, landing gear, flaps, and the flap indicator. We'll need a check list for landing, but we'll get that on the radio . . . Well, maybe we'd better tell the world about our problems. [*To* STEWARDESS.] Do you know how to work this radio? They've added a lot of gizmos since my flying days.

STEWARDESS [*pointing*]: It's this panel up here they use to talk to the ground, but I'm not sure which switches you have to set.

SPENCER: Ah yes, here's the channel selector. Maybe we'd better leave it where it is. Oh, and here we are— "transmit." [*He flicks a switch and a small light glows on the radio control panel.*] Now we're in business. [*He picks up the mike and headset beside him, then turns to the other two.*] Look, whatever happens I'm going to need another pair of hands here. Doc, I guess you'll be needed back with the others, so I think the best choice is Miss Canada here. How about it?

STEWARDESS: But I know nothing about all this!

SPENCER: Then that'll make us a real good pair. But I'll tell you what to do ahead of time. Better get in that other seat and strap yourself in. That all right with you, Doc?

BAIRD: Yes, do that. I'll take care of things in the back. And I'd better go there now. Good luck!

SPENCER: Good luck to *you*. We're all going to need it.

[BAIRD *exits.*]

SPENCER: What's your first name?

STEWARDESS: Janet.

SPENCER: Okay, Janet. Let's see if I can remember how to send out a distress message . . . Better put on that headset beside you. [*Into mike.*] Mayday! Mayday! Mayday! [*To* STEWARDESS.] What's our flight number?

STEWARDESS: 714.

SPENCER [*into mike*]: This is Flight 714, Maple

Leaf Air Charter, in distress. Come in anyone. Over.

VOICE ON RADIO [*immediately, crisply*]: This is Calgary, 714. Go ahead!

VOICE ON RADIO (VANCOUVER OPERATOR): Vancouver here, 714. All other aircraft stay off the air. Over.

SPENCER: Thank you, Calgary and Vancouver. This message is for Vancouver. This aircraft is in distress. Both pilots and some passengers . . . [*To* STEWARDESS.] How many passengers?

STEWARDESS: It was seven a few minutes ago. It may be more now.

SPENCER: Correction. At least seven passengers are suffering from food poisoning. Both pilots are unconscious and in serious condition. We have a doctor on board who says that neither pilot can be revived. Did you get that, Vancouver? [*Pause.*] Now we come to the interesting bit. My name is Spencer, George Spencer. I am a passenger on this airplane. Correction: I *was* a passenger. I have about a thousand hours' total flying time, but all of it was on single-engine fighters. And also I haven't flown an airplane for ten years. Now then, Vancouver, you'd better get someone on this radio who can give me some instructions about flying this machine. Our altitude is 16,000, course 290 magnetic, air speed 210 knots. We are on automatic pilot. Your move, Vancouver. Over. [*To* STEWARDESS.] You want to take a bet that that stirred up a little flurry down below?

[*The* STEWARDESS *shakes her head, but does not reply.*

[DISSOLVE TO: *the Control Room, Vancouver. The* CONTROLLER *is putting down a phone as the* RADIO OPERATOR *brings a message to him. He reads the message.*]

CONTROLLER: Oh, no! [*To* RADIO OPERATOR.] Ask if . . . No, let me talk to them.

[CONTROLLER *goes to panel and takes the transmitter mike. The* RADIO OPERATOR *turns a switch and nods.*]

CONTROLLER [*tensely*]: Flight 714. This is Vancouver Control. Please check with your doctor on board for any possibility of either pilot recovering. Ask him to do everything possible to revive one of the pilots, even if it means neglecting other people. Over.

SPENCER'S VOICE ON RADIO: Vancouver, this is 714, Spencer speaking. I understand your message. But the doctor says there is no possibility whatever of either pilot recovering to make the landing. He says they are critically ill and may die unless they get hospital treatment soon. Over.

CONTROLLER: All right, 714. Stand by, please. [*He pauses momentarily to consider the next course of action. Then briskly to* SWITCHBOARD OPERATOR.] Get me area traffic control—fast. [*Into phone.*] Vancouver Controller. The emergency we had!—right now it looks like it's shaping up for a disaster.

[FADE OUT]

ACT III

FADE IN: *the Control Room, Vancouver. The atmosphere is one of restrained pandemonium. The* RADIO OPERATOR *is typing a message. The teletypes are busy. The* CONTROLLER *is on one telephone and* HARRY BURDICK *on another. During what follows cut back and forth from one to the other.*

CONTROLLER [*into phone*]: As of right now, hold everything taking off for the east. You've got 45 minutes to clear any traffic for south, west or north. After that, hold everything that's scheduled outwards. On incoming traffic, accept anything you can get on the deck within the next 45 minutes. Anything you can't get down by then for sure, divert away from this area. Hold it. [*A* MESSENGER *hands him a message, which he scans. Then to* MESSENGER.] Tell the security officer. [*Into phone.*] If you've any flights coming in from the Pacific, divert them to Seattle. And any traffic inland is to stay well away from the east-west lane between Calgary and Vancouver. Got that? Right.

BURDICK [*into phone*]: Is that Cross-Canada Airlines? . . . Who's on duty in operations? . . . Let me talk to him. [*Pause.*] Mr. Gardner, it's Harry Burdick of Maple Leaf Charter. We have incoming flight that's in bad trouble and we need an experienced pilot to talk on the radio. Someone who's flown DC-4's. Can you help us? [*Pause.*] Captain Treleaven? Yes, I know him well. [*Pause.*] You mean he's with you now? [*Pause.*] Can he come over to Control right away? [*Pause.*] Thank you. Thank you very much. [*To* SWITCHBOARD OPERATOR.] Get me Montreal. I want to talk with Mr. Barney Whitmore. You may have to try Maple Leaf Air Charter office first, and someone there'll have his home number. Tell them the call is urgent.

SWITCHBOARD OPERATOR: Right. [*To* CONTROLLER.] I've got the fire chief.

CONTROLLER [*into phone*]: Chief, we have an emergency. It's Flight 714, due here at 0505. It may be a crash landing. Have everything you've got stand by. If you have men off duty call them in. Take your instructions from the Tower. They'll tell you which runway we're using. And notify the city fire department. They may want to move equipment into this area. Right. [*To* SWITCHBOARD OPERATOR.] Now get me the city police again—Inspector Moyse.

SWITCHBOARD OPERATOR: I have Seattle and Calgary waiting. They both received the message from Flight 714 and want to know if we got it clearly.

CONTROLLER: Tell them thank you, yes, and we're working the aircraft direct. But ask them to keep a listening watch in case we run into any reception trouble. [*Another message is handed him. After reading, he passes it to* BURDICK.] There's bad weather moving in. That's all we need. [*To* SWITCHBOARD OPERATOR.] Have you got the police? Right! [*Into phone.*] It's the Airport Controller again, Inspector. We're in bad trouble and we may have a crash landing. We'll need every spare ambulance in the city out here—and doctors and nurses too. Will you arrange it? [*Pause.*] Yes, we do—

56 passengers and a crew of three. [*Pause.*] Yes, the same time—0505. That's less than three hours.

BURDICK [*to* SWITCHBOARD]: Is Montreal on the line yet? Yes, give it to me. Hullo. Hullo. Is that you, Barney? It's Harry Burdick in Vancouver. I'll give you this fast, Barney. Our flight from Toronto is in bad trouble. They have food poisoning on board and both pilots and a lot of the passengers have passed out. There's a doctor on board and he says there's no chance of recovery before they get to hospital. [*Pause.*] It's a passenger doing the flying. He's just been on the radio. [*Pause.*] No, he isn't qualified. He flew single-engine fighters in the war, nothing since. [*Pause.*] I've asked him that. This doctor on board says there isn't a chance. [*Pause.*] What else can we do? We've got to talk him down. Cross-Canada are lending us a pilot. It's Captain Treleaven, one of their senior men. He's here now, just arrived. We'll get on the radio with a check list and try to bring him in. [*Pause.*] We'll do the best we can. [*Pause. Then impatiently.*] Of course it's a terrible risk, but can you think of something better? [*Pause.*] No, the papers aren't on to it yet, but don't worry, they will be soon. We can't help that now. [*Pause. Anxious to get off phone.*] That's all we know, Barney. It only just happened, I called you right away. ETA is 0505 Pacific time; that's just under two hours. I've got a lot to do, Barney. I'll have to get on with it. [*Pause. Nodding impatiently.*] I'll call you. I'll call you as soon as I know anything more . . . G'bye. [*During the foregoing* CAPTAIN MARTIN TRELEAVEN, *45, has entered. He is wearing airline uniform. As* BURDICK *sees* TRELEAVEN, *he beckons him, indicating that he should listen. To* TRELEAVEN.] Did you get that?

TRELEAVEN [*calmly*]: Is that the whole story?

BURDICK: That's everything we know. Now what I want you to do is get on the horn and talk this pilot down. You'll have to help him get the feel of the airplane on the way. You'll have to talk him round the circuit. You'll have to give him the cockpit check for landing, and—so help me!—you'll have to talk him on to the ground.

[CAPTAIN TRELEAVEN *is a calm man, not easily perturbed. While* BURDICK *has been talking, the* CAPTAIN *has been filling his pipe. Now, with methodical movements, he puts away his tobacco pouch and begins to light the pipe.*]

TRELEAVEN [*quietly*]: You realize, of course, that the chances of a man who has only flown fighter airplanes landing a four-engine passenger ship safely are about nine to one against.

BURDICK [*rattled*]: Of course I know it! You heard what I told Whitmore. But do *you* have any other ideas?

TRELEAVEN: No. I just wanted to be sure you knew what we are getting into, Harry. All right. Let's get started. Where do I go?

CONTROLLER: Over here.

[*They cross to the radio panel and the* OPERATOR *hands him the last message from the aircraft. When he has read it he takes the transmitter mike.*]

TRELEAVEN: How does this thing work?

RADIO OPERATOR [*turning a switch*]: You're on the air now.

TRELEAVEN [*calmly*]: Hullo, Flight 714. This is Vancouver and my name is Martin Treleaven. I am a Cross-Canada Airlines captain and my job right now is to help fly this airplane in. First of all, are you hearing me okay? Over.

VOICE OF SPENCER: Yes, Captain, loud and clear. Go ahead, please.

TRELEAVEN: Where's the message? [*As* OPERATOR *passes it. Into mike.*] I see that I'm talking to George Spencer. Well, George, I don't think you're going to have much trouble. These DC-4s handle easily, and we'll give you the drill for landing. But first of all, please tell me what your flying experience is. The message says you have flown single-engine fighters. What kind of airplanes were these, and did you fly multi-engine airplanes at all? Let's hear from you, George. Over.

[CUT TO: *the flight deck.*]

SPENCER [*into mike*]: Hullo, Vancouver, this is 714. Glad to have you along, Captain. But let's not kid each other, please. We both know we need a lot of luck. About my flying. It was mostly on Spitfires and Mustangs. And I have around a thousand hours total. And all that was ten years ago. Over.

[CUT TO: *the Control Room.*]

TRELEAVEN [*into mike*]: Don't worry about that, George. It's like riding a bicycle. You never forget it. Stand by.

CONTROLLER [*to* TRELEAVEN]: The air force has picked up the airplane on radar and they'll be giving us courses to bring him in. [*Hands over paper.*] Here's the first one. See if you can get him on that heading.

TRELEAVEN [*nods; then into mike*]: 714, are you still on automatic pilot? If so, look for the auto-pilot release switch. It's a push-button on the control yoke and is plainly marked. Over.

[CUT TO: *the flight deck.*]

SPENCER [*into mike*]: Yes, Vancouver. I see the auto-pilot switch. Over.

[CUT TO: *the Control Room.*]

TRELEAVEN [*into mike*]: Now, George, in a minute you can unlock the automatic pilot and get the feel of the controls, and we're going to change your course a little. But first listen carefully. When you use the controls they will seem very heavy and sluggish compared with a fighter airplane. But don't worry, that's quite normal. You must take care, though, to watch your air speed carefully and do not let it fall below 120 knots while your wheels and flaps are up. Otherwise you will stall. Now, do you have someone up there who can work the radio to leave you free for flying? Over.

[CUT TO: *the flight deck.*]

SPENCER [*into mike*]: Yes, Vancouver. I have the stewardess here with me and she will take over the radio now. I am going to unlock the automatic pilot. Over. [*To* STEWARDESS *as he depresses the auto-pilot release.*] Well, here we go.

[*Feeling the controls,* SPENCER *eases into a left*

turn. Then, straightening out, he eases the control column slightly forward and back.

[CUT TO: *the Control Room.*]

TRELEAVEN'S VOICE: Hullo, 714. How are you making out, George? Have you got the feel of her yet?

[CUT TO: *the flight deck.*]

SPENCER. Tell him I'm on manual now and trying out some gentle turns.

STEWARDESS [*into mike*]: Hullo, Vancouver. We are on manual now and trying out some gentle turns.

[CUT TO: *the Control Room.*]

TRELEAVEN [*into mike*]: Hullo, George Spencer. Try the effect of fore-and-aft control on your air speed. To begin with, close your throttles slightly and bring your air speed back to 160. Adjust the trim as you go along. But watch that air speed closely. Remember to keep it well above 120. Over.

[CUT TO: *the flight deck.*]

SPENCER [*tensely. Still feeling out the controls*]: Tell him okay.

STEWARDESS [*into mike*]: Okay, Vancouver. We are doing as you say.

TRELEAVEN'S VOICE [*after a pause*]: Hullo, 714. How does she handle, George?

SPENCER [*disgustedly*]: Tell him sluggish like a wet sponge.

STEWARDESS: Sluggish like a wet sponge, Vancouver.

[CUT TO: *the Control Room. There is a momentary relaxing of tension as* CAPTAIN TRELEAVEN *and the group around him exchange grins.*]

TRELEAVEN [*into mike*]: Hullo, George Spencer. That would be a natural feeling because you were used to handling smaller airplanes. The thing you have got to remember is that there is a bigger lag in the effect of control movements on air speed, compared with what you were used to before. Do you understand that? Over.

[CUT TO: *the flight deck.*]

SPENCER: Tell him I understand.

STEWARDESS [*into mike*]: Hullo, Vancouver. Yes, he understands. Over.

[CUT TO: *the Control Room*.]

TRELEAVEN [*into mike*]: Hullo, George Spencer. Because of that lag in air speed you must avoid any violent movements of the controls, such as you used to make in your fighter airplanes. If you *do* move the controls violently, you will overcorrect and be in trouble. Is that understood? Over.

[CUT TO: *the flight deck*.]

SPENCER [*nodding, beginning to perspire*]: Tell him —yes, I understand.

STEWARDESS [*into mike*]: Yes, Vancouver. Your message is understood. Over.

[CUT TO: *the Control Room*.]

TRELEAVEN [*into mike*]: Hullo, George Spencer. Now I want you to feel how the ship handles at lower speeds when the flaps and wheels are down. But don't do anything until I give you the instructions. Is that clear? Over.

[CUT TO: *the flight deck*.]

SPENCER: Tell him okay: let's have the instructions.

STEWARDESS [*into mike*]: Hullo, Vancouver. Yes, we understand. Go ahead with the instructions. Over.

TRELEAVEN'S VOICE: First of all, throttle back slightly, get your air speed steady at 160 knots, and adjust your trim to maintain level flight. Then tell me when you're ready. Over.

SPENCER: Watch that air speed, Janet. You'll have to call it off to me when we land, so you may as well start practising.

STEWARDESS: It's 200 now . . . 190 . . . 185 . . . 180 . . . 175 . . . 175 . . . 165 . . . 155 . . . 150 . . . [*Alarmed*.] That's too low! He said 160!

SPENCER [*tensely*]: I know. I know. Watch it! It's that lag on the air speed I can't get used to.

STEWARDESS: 150 . . . 150 . . . 155 . . . 160 . . . 160 . . . It's steady on 160.

SPENCER: Tell them.

STEWARDESS [*into mike*]: Hullo Vancouver. This is 714. Our speed is steady at 160. Over.

[CUT TO: *the Control Room*.]

TRELEAVEN [*into mike*]: Okay, 714. Now, George, I want you to put down 20 degrees of flap. But be careful not to make it any more. The flap lever is at the base of the control pedestal and is plainly marked. Twenty degrees will mean moving the lever down to the second notch. Over.

[CUT TO: *the flight deck.*]

SPENCER: Janet, *you'll* have to put the flaps down. [*Pointing.*] There's the lever.

TRELEAVEN'S VOICE: Can you see the flap indicator, George? It's near the centre of the main panel.

SPENCER: Here's the indicator he's talking about. When I tell you, push the lever down to the second notch and watch the dial. Okay?

STEWARDESS: Okay. [*Then with alarm.*] Oh, look at the air speed! It's down to 125!

[SPENCER *grimaces and pushes the control column forward.*]

SPENCER [*urgently*]: Call off the speed! Call off the speed!

STEWARDESS: 140 . . . 150 . . . 160 . . . 170 . . . 175 . . . Can't you get back to 160?

SPENCER [*straining*]: I'm trying! I'm trying! [*Pause.*] There it is.

[CUT TO: *the passenger cabin.*]

SECOND WOMAN PASSENGER [*frightened*]: Hector! Hector! We're going to crash! I know it! Oh, do something! Do something!

BAIRD [*he appears at her elbow*]: Have her take this. It'll help calm her down. [*Gives pill and cup to* THIRD MALE PASSENGER.] Try not to worry. That young man at the front is a very experienced pilot. He's just what they call "getting the feel" of the airplane. [*He moves aft in the cabin.*]

FIRST MALE PASSENGER: Doctor!

BAIRD: Yes.

FIRST MALE PASSENGER: Tell us the truth, Doctor. Have we got a chance? Does this fellow know how to fly this thing?

BAIRD: We've got all kinds of chances. He's a very

experienced pilot, but it's just that he's not used to flying this particular type and he's getting the feel of it.

FOURTH MALE PASSENGER: You didn't need none of them pills to make me sick. Never mind me dinner. Now Ah'm worried about yesterday's breakfast.

[CUT TO: *the flight deck*.]

STEWARDESS [*into mike*]: Hullo, Vancouver. Air speed is 160 and we are ready to put down the flaps. Over.

[CUT TO: *the Control Room*.]

TRELEAVEN [*into mike*]: Okay, 714. Go ahead with your flaps. But be careful—only 20 degrees. Then, when you have 20 degrees down, bring back the air speed to 140, adjust your trim, and call me again. Over.

[CUT TO: *the flight deck*.]

SPENCER: Okay, Janet—flaps down! 20 degrees. [*The* STEWARDESS *pushes down the flap lever to its second notch*.] Tell them we've got the flaps down, and the air speed's coming to 140.

STEWARDESS [*into mike*]: Hullo, Vancouver. This is 714. The flaps are down and our air speed is 140.

[CUT TO: *the Control Room*.]

TRELEAVEN: All right, 714. Now the next thing is to put the wheels down. Are you still maintaining level flight?

[CUT TO: *the flight deck*.]

SPENCER: Tell him—more or less.

STEWARDESS [*into mike*]: Hullo, Vancouver. More or less.

[CUT TO: *the Control Room*.]

RADIO OPERATOR: This guy's got a sense of humour.

BURDICK: That's a *real* help.

TRELEAVEN [*into mike*]: Okay, 714. Try to keep your altitude steady and your speed at 140. Then when you *are* ready, put down the landing gear and let your speed come back to 120. You will have to advance your throttle setting to maintain that air speed, and also adjust your trim. Is that understood? Over.

[CUT TO: *the flight deck*.]

SPENCER: Ask him—what about the propeller controls and mixture?

STEWARDESS [*into mike*]: Hullo Vancouver. What about the propeller controls and mixture? Over.

[CUT TO: *the Control Room.*]

CONTROLLER: He's thinking, anyway.

TRELEAVEN [*into mike*]: Leave them alone for the time being. Just concentrate on holding that air speed steady with the wheels and flaps down. Over.

[CUT TO: *the flight deck.*]

SPENCER: Wheels down, Janet, and call off the air speed.

STEWARDESS [*Puts landing gear down*]: 140 . . . 145 . . . 140 . . . 135 . . . 130 . . . 125 . . . 120 . . . 115 . . . The speed's too low!

SPENCER: Keep calling it!!

STEWARDESS: 115 . . . 120 . . . 120 . . . Steady on 120.

[CUT TO: *the Control Room.*]

TRELEAVEN [*into mike*]: Hullo, George Spencer. Your wheels should be down by now and look for three green lights to show that they're locked. Over.

[CUT TO: *the flight deck.*]

SPENCER: Are they on?

STEWARDESS: Yes—all three lights are green.

SPENCER: Tell them.

STEWARDESS [*into mike*]: Hullo, Vancouver. Yes, there are three green lights.

[CUT TO: *the Control Room.*]

TRELEAVEN: Okay, 714, now let's put down full flap so that you can feel how the airplane will handle when you're landing. As soon as full flap is down, bring your air speed back to 110 knots and trim to hold it steady. Adjust your throttle setting to hold your altitude. Is that understood? Over.

[CUT TO: *the flight deck.*]

SPENCER: Tell him "yes."

STEWARDESS [*into mike*]: Yes, Vancouver. That is understood.

SPENCER: Full flap, Janet! Push the lever all the way down, and call off the air speed.

STEWARDESS: 120 . . . 115 . . . 115 . . . 110 . . . 110 . . .

SPENCER: Okay, tell 'em we've got full flap and air speed 110, and she still handles like a sponge, only more so.

STEWARDESS [*into mike*]: Hullo, Vancouver. We have full flap, and air speed is 110. And the pilot says she still handles like a sponge, only more so.

[CUT TO: *the Control Room. Again there is a momentary sense of relief.*]

TRELEAVEN [*into mike*]: That's nice going, George. Now I'm going to give you instructions for holding your height and air speed while you raise the flaps and landing gear. Then we'll run through the whole procedure again.

[CUT TO: *the flight deck.*]

SPENCER: Again! I don't know if my nerves'll stand it.

[*Pause.*]

All right. Tell him okay.

[DISSOLVE TO: *Control Room clock showing 2:55.*]

[DISSOLVE TO: *Control Room clock showing 5:20.*]

[DISSOLVE TO: *the Control Room.* CAPTAIN TRELEAVEN *is still seated in front of the transmiter, but has obviously been under strain. He now has his coat off and his tie loosened and there is an empty carton of coffee beside him.* BURDICK *and the* CONTROLLER *are in background, watching tensely. A phone rings and the* CONTROLLER *answers it. He makes a note and passes it to* TRELEAVEN.]

TRELEAVEN [*into mike*]: Hullo Flight 714. Our flying practice has slowed you down and you are later than we expected. You are now 12 minutes' flying time from Vancouver Airport, but it's getting light, so your landing will be in daylight. You should be able to see us at any minute. Do you see the airport beacon? Over.

STEWARDESS' VOICE: Yes, we see the airport beacon. Over.

TRELEAVEN: Okay George, now you've practised everything we need for a landing. You've flown the ship with wheels and flaps down, and you know how she handles. Your fuel feeds are checked and you're all set to come in. You won't hear from me again for a few minutes because I'm moving to the Control Tower so I'll be able to see you on the circuit and approach. Is that clear? Over.

STEWARDESS' VOICE: Yes, Vancouver, that is understood. Over.

TRELEAVEN: All right, George. Continue to approach at two thousand feet on your present heading and wait for instructions. We'll let you know the runway to use at the last minute because the wind is shifting. Don't forget we want you to do at least one dummy run, and then go round again so you'll have practice in making the landing approach. Over.

[*He mops his forehead with a crumpled handkerchief.*]

[CUT TO: *the flight deck.* SPENCER, *too, has his coat off and tie loosened. His hair is ruffled and the strain is plainly beginning to tell on him. The* STEWARDESS *is still in the co-pilot's seat and* BAIRD *is standing behind them both. The* STEWARDESS *is about to acknowledge the last radio message, but* SPENCER *stops her.*]

SPENCER: I'll take it, Janet.

[*Into mike.*]

No dice, Vancouver. We're coming straight in and the first time is "it." Dr. Baird is here beside me. He reports two of the passengers and the First Officer are in critical condition, and we must land in the next few minutes. The doctor asks that you have stomach pumps and oxygen equipment ready. Over.

[CUT TO: *the Control Room.*]

BURDICK. He mustn't! We need time!

TRELEAVEN. It's his decision. By all the rules he's in command of the airplane.

[*Into mike.*]

714, your message is understood. Good luck to us all. Listening out.

[*To* BURDICK *and* CONTROLLER.]

Let's go!

[DISSOLVE TO: *the flight deck.*]

SPENCER: This is it, Doctor. You'd better go back now and make sure everybody's strapped in tight. Are both the pilots in seats?

BAIRD: Yes.

SPENCER: How about the passengers who aren't sick? Are they worried?

BAIRD: A little, but there's no panic. I exaggerated your qualifications. I'd better go. Good luck.

SPENCER [*with ironic grin*]: Thanks.

[DISSOLVE TO: *the Control Tower, Vancouver Airport. It is a glass-enclosed area, with radio panels and other equipment, and access is by a stairway from below. It is now daylight and the* TOWER CONTROLLER *is looking skywards, using binoculars. There is the sound of hurried feet on the stairway and* TRELEAVEN, *the* CONTROLLER *and* BURDICK *emerge in that order.*]

TOWER CONTROLLER: There he is!

[TRELEAVEN *picks up a second pair of binoculars, looks through them quickly, then puts them down.*]

TRELEAVEN: All right—let's make our decision on the runway. What's it to be?

TOWER CONTROLLER: Zero eight. It's pretty well into wind now, though there'll be a slight cross-wind from the right. It's also the longest.

TRELEAVEN [*into mike*]: Hullo, Flight 714. This is Martin Treleaven in Vancouver Tower. Do you read me? Over.

[CUT TO: *the flight deck.*]

STEWARDESS [*into mike*]: Yes, Vancouver Tower. Loud and clear. Over.

[CUT TO: *the Tower.*]

TRELEAVEN [*crisply, authoritatively, yet calmly*]: From here on, do not acknowledge any further transmissions unless you wish to ask a question. You are now ready to join the airport circuit. The runway for landing is zero eight. That means you are now cross-wind and will shortly make a left turn on to the down-wind leg. Begin now to lose height to one thousand feet. Throttle back slightly and make your descent at 400 feet a minute. Let your air speed come back to 160 knots and hold it steady there . . . Air speed 160.

CONTROLLER [*reaching for phone*]: Runway is zero eight. All vehicles stand by near the extreme south end. Do not, repeat not, go down the runway until the aircraft has passed by you because it may swing off. Is that clear? [*Pause.*] Right.

[CUT TO: FILM INSERT—*fire trucks and ambulances are manned and move away with sirens wailing.*]

[CUT TO: *the flight deck.* SPENCER *is pushing the throttles forward and the tempo of the motors increases.*]

SPENCER: Tell them we're at one thousand feet and levelling off.

STEWARDESS [*into mike*]: Vancouver Tower. We are now at one thousand feet and levelling off. Over.

TRELEAVEN'S VOICE: Now let's have 20 degrees of flap. Do not acknowledge this message.

SPENCER: 20 degrees of flap, Janet.

[*The* STEWARDESS *reaches for flap lever and pushes it down while she watches the flap indicator.*]

TRELEAVEN'S VOICE: When you have your flaps down, bring your air speed back slowly to 140 knots, adjust your trim, and begin to make a left turn on to the down-wind leg. When you have turned, fly parallel with the runway you see on your left. I repeat—air speed 140 and begin a left turn.

[CUT TO: *close-up of instrument panel showing artificial horizon and air-speed indicator. The air speed first comes back to 140, goes slightly below it, then returns to 140. The artificial horizon tilts so that the airplane symbol is banked to the left.*]

[CUT TO: *the flight deck.* SPENCER *has control yoke turned to the left and is adjusting the throttles.*]

[CUT TO: *the Tower.*]

TRELEAVEN: Watch our height! Don't make that turn so steep! Watch your height! More throttle! Keep

the air speed on 140 and the nose up! Get back that
height! You need a thousand feet!

[CUT TO: *the flight deck.* SPENCER *eases the throttles open and the tempo of the motors increases.
He eases the control column forward, then pulls
back again.*

[CUT TO: *close-up of a climb and descent indicator. The instrument first shows a descent of 500-
feet-per-minute drop, then a climb of 600 feet, and
then gradually begins to level off.*

[CUT TO: *the Control Tower.* CAPTAIN TRELEAV-
EN *is looking out through binoculars, the others
anxiously behind him.*]

TRELEAVEN [*angrily*]: He can't fly the bloody thing!
Of course he can't fly it! You're watching fifty people
going to their deaths!

BURDICK [*shouting*]: Keep talking to him! Keep
talking! Tell him what to do!

TRELEAVEN [*urgently, into mike*]: Spencer, you
can't come straight in! You've got to do some circuits,
and practise that approach. You've enough fuel left for
three hours' flying. Stay up, man! Stay up!

[CUT TO: *the flight deck.*]

SPENCER: Give it to me! [*Taking the mike. Then
tensely.*] Listen, down there! I'm coming in! Do you
hear me?—I'm coming in. There are people up here
who'll die in less than an hour, never mind three. I may
bend your precious airplane a bit, but I'll get it down.
Now get on with the landing check. I'm putting the gear
down now. [*To* STEWARDESS.] Wheels down, Janet!

[*The* STEWARDESS *selects landing gear "down" and
SPENCER reaches for the throttles.*

[CUT TO: *airplane in flight, daylight. Its landing
wheels come down.*

[CUT TO: *the flight deck.*]

STEWARDESS [*looks out of window, then back to
SPENCER*]: Wheels down and three green lights.

[CUT TO: *the Tower.*]

BURDICK: He may not be able to fly worth a damn,
but he's sure got guts.

TRELEAVEN [*into mike*]: Increase your throttle setting slightly to hold your air speed now that the wheels are down. Adjust your trim and keep that height at a thousand feet. Now check your propeller setting and your mixture—propellers to fully fine; mixture to full rich. I'll repeat that. Propellers to fully fine; mixture to full rich.

[CUT TO: *the flight deck*.]

SPENCER [*to himself, as he moves controls*]: Propellers fully fine. Mixture full rich. [*To* STEWARDESS.] Janet, let me hear the air speed.

STEWARDESS: 130 . . . 125 . . . 120 . . . 125 . . . 130 . . .

[CUT TO: *the Tower*.]

TRELEAVEN [*into mike*]: You are well down-wind now. You can begin to make a left turn on the crosswind leg. As you turn, begin losing height to 800 feet and let your air speed come back to 120. I'll repeat that. Start a left turn. Lose height to 800. Air speed 120. [*He picks up binoculars, then puts them down hurriedly and takes mike again.*] You are losing height too fast! You are losing height too fast! Open up! Open! Hold your height now! Keep your air speed at 120.

[CUT TO: *the flight deck*.]

STEWARDESS: 110 . . . 110 . . . 105 . . . 110 . . . 110 . . . 120 . . . 120 . . . Steady at 120.

SPENCER: What a miserable insensitive wagon this is! It doesn't respond! It doesn't respond at all!

STEWARDESS: 125 . . . 130 . . . 130 . . . Steady on 130.

[CUT TO: *the Tower*.]

TRELEAVEN: Start your turn into wind now to line up with the runway. Make it a gentle turn—you've plenty of time. As you turn, begin losing height, about 400 feet a minute. But be ready to correct if you lose height too fast. Adjust your trim as you go. That's right! Keep turning! As soon as you've completed the turn, put down full flap and bring your air speed to 115. I'll repeat that. Let down 400 feet a minute. Full flap. Then air speed 115. [*To the others.*] Is everything ready on the field?

CONTROLLER: As ready as we'll ever be.

TRELEAVEN: Then this is it. In sixty seconds we'll know.

[CUT TO: *the flight deck.*]

SPENCER [*muttering*]: Not quite yet . . . a little more . . . that should do it. [*As he straightens out of the turn.*] Janet, give me full flap! [*The* STEWARD- ESS *reaches for the flap control, pushes it down and leaves it down.*] Height and air speed!

STEWARDESS: 700 feet, speed 130 . . . 600 feet, speed 120 . . . 500 feet, speed 105 . . . We're going down too quickly!

SPENCER: I know! I know! [*He pushes throttle for- ward and the tempo of the motors increases.*] Keep watching it!

STEWARDESS: 450 feet, speed 100 . . . 400 feet, speed 100 . . .

    [CUT TO: FILM INSERT—*airplane (DC-4) with wheels and flaps down, on a landing approach.*

    [CUT TO: *the Tower.*]

TRELEAVEN [*urgently into mike*]: Open up! Open up! You're losing height too fast! [*Pause.*] Watch the air speed! Your nose is too high! Open up quickly or she'll stall! Open up, man! open up!

BURDICK: He heard you. He's recovering.

TRELEAVEN [*into mike*]: Maintain that height until you get closer in to the runway. But be ready to ease off gently . . . You can start now . . . Let down again . . . That looks about right . . . But watch the air speed. Your nose is creeping up . . . [*More steadily.*] Now listen carefully, George. There's a slight cross-wind on the runway and your drift is to the right. Straighten up just before you touch down, and be ready with more right rudder as soon as you *are* down. And remember to cut the switches if you land too fast. [*Pause.*] All right, your approach is good . . . Get ready to round out—now! [*Pause. Then urgently.*] You're coming in too fast! Lift the nose up!

    [CUT TO: *the flight deck.*]

TRELEAVEN'S VOICE: Lift the nose up! Back on the

throttles! Throttles right back! Hold her off! Not too much! Not too much! Be ready for that cross-wind! Ease her down, *now!* Ease her down!

> [CUT TO: FILM INSERT—*a landing wheel skimming over a runway and about to touch down. As it makes contact, rock picture to show instability.*
> [CUT TO: *the flight deck. There is a heavy thud and* SPENCER *and the* STEWARDESS *are jolted in their seats. There is another, another, and another. Everything shakes.*

SPENCER [*shouting*]: Cut the switches! Cut the switches!

> [*The* STEWARDESS *reaches upward and pulls down the cage of the master switches. Instantly the heavy roar of motors stops, but there is still a whistling because the airplane is travelling fast.* SPENCER *stretches out his legs as he puts his full strength into applying the airplane toe brakes, at the same time pulling back on the control column. There is a screaming of rubber on pavement, and* SPENCER *and the* STEWARDESS *are thrown violently to the left. Then, except for the hum of the radio and gyros, there is silence as the airplane stops.*]

SPENCER [*disgustedly*]: I groundlooped! I did a lousy stinking groundloop! We're turned right around the way we came!

STEWARDESS: But we're all right! We're all right! You did it! You did it!

> [*She leans over and kisses him.* SPENCER *pulls off his radio headset. Outside there is a rising note of approaching sirens. Then, from the headset we hear* CAPTAIN TRELEAVEN's *voice.*]

TRELEAVEN'S VOICE [*exuberantly*]: Hullo, George Spencer. That was probably the lousiest landing in the history of this airport. So don't ever ask us for a job as a pilot. But there are some people here who'd like to shake you by the hand, and later on we'll buy you a drink. Stay right where you are, George! We're coming over.

[FADE OUT.]

Indian

GEORGE RYGA

A large, empty set in gray noncountry.

One might therefore think of the set as being on sandy flat land, almost desert-type, with only a few suggested tufts of scraggy growth. A suggestion of distant horizon. A suggestion of two or three fenceposts, newly driven, still bare of wire, receding in the distance. In foreground, one fence post newly and not yet fully driven in. Pile of dirt around the post. Shovel, hammer.

When the Indian AGENT *enters, he actually drives in —or we cut him in already—in a big car, vintage about 1958. In the end he must start up and drive out. Maybe he can leave tracks in the sand.*

Return camera to tent and pan to right, where INDIAN *is asleep, hat on face, in short prairie grass. As camera holds on sleeper, there is sound of footsteps, and feet of the farmer approach, stopping short of* INDIAN's *head.*

WATSON [*loud and angry*]: What the hell! Come on —ya aimin' to die like that!

INDIAN [*clutching his hat and sitting up; lifts hat and looks up, then jerks hat down over face*]: Hey! The sun blind me! Boss, I am sick—head gonna explode! [*Tries to lie back.*]

WATSON [*grabbing* INDIAN's *arm and yanking him to his feet*]: There's gonna be some bigger explosions if I don't get action outa youse guys! What happened? Where's the fat boy—an' the guy with the wooden leg?

INDIAN: Jus' a minute, boss. Don't shout like that. [*Looks carefully around him.*] They not here. Guess they run away, boss—no? Roy, he not got wooden leg. He got bone leg same's you an' me—only it dried up an' look like wood. Small, too. [*Lifts up his own right leg.*] That shoe—that was fit Roy's bad leg. The other shoe is tight. But this one, she is hunder times tighter!

WATSON [*squatting*]: Is them Limpy's boots?

INDIAN: Yah. I win them at poker last night. Boss, what a time we have—everybody go haywire!

WATSON [*looks about him impatiently*]: I can see. Where's your tent?

INDIAN [*pointing to ashes*]: There she is! I never see anything burn like that before!

WATSON: The kid wasn't lyin'—you guys *did* burn the tent.

INDIAN: What kid?

WATSON: Yore kid.

INDIAN [*jumps to his feet*]: Alphonse? Where is Alphonse? He run away when Sam an' Roy start fight!

WATSON: Yeh—he came to the house. Told us how you guys got drunk an' wild. So the missus fixed him something to eat an' put him to bed.

INDIAN: He's all right! Oh, that's good, boss.

WATSON [*smiling grimly*]: Like I said, the missus fed the kid. Then I took him an' put him in the granary, lockin' the door so he ain't gonna get out. That's for protection.

INDIAN: Protection? You don't need protection, boss. Alphonse not gonna hurt you.

WATSON: Ha! Ha! Ha! Big joke! Where are yore pals, was gonna help you with this job?

INDIAN: I don't know—they run away when tent catch fire.

WATSON: That's just great! You know what you guys done? Yesterday you nicked me for ten dollars. I'm hungry—the fat boy says to me—my stomach roar like thunder. He's gonna roar plenty before I'm finished with you an' him! How much you figure the fence you put up is worth?

INDIAN [*rubbing his eyes and trying to see the fence in the distance*]: I dunno, boss. You say job is worth forty dollars. Five, mebbe ten dollars done . . .

WATSON: Five dollars! Look here, smart guy— you've got twenty-nine posts in—I counted them. At ten cents apiece, you've done two dollars ninety cents worth of work! An' you got ten dollars off me yesterday!

INDIAN [*pondering sadly*]: Looks like you in the hole, boss.

WATSON: Maybe I am, an' maybe I ain't. I got yore kid in the granary, locked up so he'll keep. You try to run off after yore pals, an' I'm gonna take my gun an' shoot a hole that big through the kid's head! [*Rings with his fingers to show exact size of injury he intends to make.*]

INDIAN: No!

WATSON: Oh, sure! So what say, Indian? You gonna work real hard and be a good boy?

INDIAN: Boss—you know me. I work! Them other guys is no good, but not Johnny. I make deal—I keep deal. You see yourself I stay when they run.

WATSON: Sure, you stayed. You were too drunk to move. What goes on in yore heads—ah, hell! You ain't worth the bother!

INDIAN: No, no, boss. You all wrong.

WATSON: Then get to work. It's half past nine, and you ain't even begun to think about the fence.

INDIAN: Boss—little bit later. I sick man—head she hurt to burst, an' stomach—ugh! Boss—I not eat anything since piece of boloney yesterday . . .

WATSON [*turning angrily*]: Go to hell—hear me? Go to hell! I got that story yesterday. Now g'wan—I wanna see some action!

INDIAN: All right, boss. You know me. You trust me.

WATSON: Trust you? I wouldn't trust you with the time of day! [*Remembering something.*] Hey! There's a snoop from the Indian Affairs department tooling around today—checking on all you guys working off the reserve. You're workin' for me—so if you got any complaints, you better tell me now. I don't want no bellyachin' to no government guys.

INDIAN: Complaints? Me? I happy, boss. What you take me for?

WATSON: Sure, sure. Now get back to work. An' remember what I told you—try to beat it, an' I shoot the kid. Understand?

INDIAN [*removing his hat and wiping his brow*]: Sure, boss. I understand.

[WATSON *leaves, and* INDIAN *looks towards the fence in the fields. Still a little unsteady, the* INDIAN *makes his way over to the nearest (unfinished) fencepost. Retrieves an old box, finds the twenty-pound hammer, approaches pole but sits a moment on the box, hammer across his knees, and rubs his eyes and forehead.*]

INDIAN: Sementos! But the head she is big today. Head hurt. Stomach, she is slopbucket full of turpentine. Two dollars a quart, Sam Cardinal says—with four dollars we get enough bad whisky to poison every Indian from here to Lac la Biche! You get one quart wood alcohol—mebbe half-quart Formalin, an' the rest is water! That's kind whisky they make for Indian. [INDIAN *gets up on box and starts to drive the post into the ground. Stops after a few seconds. Winded.*] Sementos! When you work for Mr. Watson you work hard. Oh—that party we have. Sam Cardinal sing like sick cow, an' Roy McIntosh dance on his bad leg. Funny! Alphonse and I laugh until stomach ache. I won Roy's boots in poker but he dance anyhow. Then Sam gets mad and he push Roy, Roy push him back. *They fight.* [INDIAN *hits the post a few times more, trying to summon up strength to get on with the work. Tosses the hammer down angrily and comes down off the box. Sits heavily, back to the post. Rubs stomach.*] Boy, I hungry. Worse than yesterday. Sam talk to Mr. Watson, get ten dollars for grub. Buy whisky, buy boloney an' two watermelon. He already eat most of boloney and I see him give hunk to friendly dog. I kick dog. Sam get mad. Why you do that

—dog do nothing to you? I say he eat my grub. He can go catch cat if he hungry. I eat cat once myself—winter 1956. Not much meat an' tough like rope, I never eat cat again. Sementos, but the head hurt. [INDIAN *gets up and retrieves the hammer.*] Scared talk. World is full of scared talk. I show scare, an' I get job from Mr. Watson. A scared Indian is a live Indian. My head don't get Alphonse out free—but hands do. [*Climbs on box and is about to strike post. We hear sound of car.*] Hello. I am big man today. First Mr. Watson—an' now car come to see me. If I not get outa way, he gonna hit me, sure as hell!

> [*Gets off box and watches. Car stops alongside him. Lettering on door reads "Department of Indian Affairs."*]

AGENT [*stepping out of car*]: Hi there, fella! How's it going?

INDIAN: Hello, mister—everything is going one hundred fifty percent! [*Rises on box and lifts hammer to drive post.*]

AGENT: I saw a burned-out camp back at the road . . . everything O.K.?

INDIAN: Sure, everything O.K. You want complaints?

AGENT: What do you mean?

INDIAN: I just say, if you want complaints, I give you lots. My tent, she is burn down last night. My partners —they run away—leave me to do big job myself. I not got money, and boss, he's got my Alphonse ready to shoot if I try run. You want more complaints? [*Drives hard on hammer and groans.*] Mebbe you want know how my head she hurts inside?

AGENT [*relieved*]: Hey, c'mere! I'll give you a smoke to make you feel better—you're in rough shape, boy! What do you want—pipe tobacco or cigarette? I got both.

INDIAN [*drops hammer and comes down from box*]: The way I feel, I could smoke old stocking full of straw. Gimme cigarette! [*Examines cigarette given him.*] You make lotsa money from guvment, boss—to-

bacco here, an' cotton there—some cigarette? Which
end you light? [*Laughs.*]

AGENT: Light whichever end you want—you can eat
it for all I care. That's some hat—where'd you get it?

INDIAN [*accepting light*]: Win at poker, mister.

AGENT [*examining him closely*]: Aren't those boots
tight? I suppose you stole them!

INDIAN: No, boss. Poker.

AGENT: And that shirt—look at it. Have shirt, will
travel!

INDIAN: I steal that from my brother, when he sick
an' dying. He never catch me.

AGENT [*laughs and wipes his eyes*]: That's good! I
must tell the boys about you—what's your name?

INDIAN: You think is funny me steal shirt from my
brother when he die? You think that funny, bossman? I
think you lousy. You think that funny, too?

AGENT [*taken back*]: Hold on now—what did you
say?

INDIAN: You hear what I say.

AGENT [*takes out notebook*]: Just give me your
name, and we'll settle with you later.

INDIAN: Turn around an' walk to road. If you want
see me steal, I steal wheels off your car. You try to
catch me.

AGENT [*angrily*]: Give me your name!

INDIAN: Maybe I forget—maybe I got no name at
all.

AGENT: Look here, boy—don't give me any backtalk
or I might have to turn a report in on you, and next time
Indian benefits are given out, yours might be hard to
claim!

INDIAN: So, you got no name for me. How you gonna
report me when you not know who I am? You want
name? All right, I give you name. Write down—Joe
Bush!

AGENT: I haven't got all day, fella. Are you, or are
you not going to tell me your name?

INDIAN: No, I never tell you, mister. It make you
scared you should know too much about me.

AGENT [*slamming book shut angrily*]: That does it! By God, if I have to go after you myself, I'm gonna find out who you are!

INDIAN: Don't get mad, boss—I sorry for what I say. I got such hurting head, I don't know what I say.

AGENT: Been drinking, eh? What was it this time—homebrew, or shaving lotion?

INDIAN: Maybe homebrew—maybe coffee, I don't know. Why you ask me?

AGENT: You know as well as I do. Besides, bad liquor's going to kill you sooner than anything else.

INDIAN [*excitedly*]: You believe that? You really mean what you say?

AGENT: What? About bad liquor—sure I do!

INDIAN: Then get me bottle good, clean Canadian whisky! I never drink clean whisky in my life!

AGENT: Come on now—you're as . . .

INDIAN: I give you twenty dollars for bottle!

AGENT: Stop it! Boy, you must have something more than a hangover wrong in your head!

INDIAN: That car yours?

AGENT: Yes.

INDIAN: How come all that writing—but your name not on it? Why you not tell truth?

AGENT: Well, I work for the government, and they provide us . . .

INDIAN: Thirty dollars!

AGENT: Look here . . .

INDIAN: How come you not in big city with office job? How come you drive around an' talk to dirty, stupid Indian? You not have much school, or mebbe something else wrong with you to have such bad job.

AGENT: Shut up, you lousy—

INDIAN: Thirty-five dollars! No more!

AGENT: Will you shut up?

INDIAN [*defiantly*]: No! I not shut up! You not man at all—you cheap woman who love for money! Your mother was woman pig, an' your father man dog.

AGENT [*startled and frightened*]: What . . . what are you saying?

INDIAN [*coming up face to face with* AGENT]: You wanna hit me? Come on—hit me! You kill me easy, an' they arrest you—same people who give you car. Hit me—even little bit—come on! You coward! Just hit me like this. [*Slaps palms together.*] Come on. You know what I do?

AGENT [*looking apprehensively around him*]: What?

INDIAN: I go report you for beating Indian, and you lose job. Come on—show me you are man! [*Dances provocatively around* AGENT.]

AGENT [*turning to his car*]: I'm getting out of here —you're crazy!

INDIAN [*jumps on front bumper of car*]: No. You not go nowhere! Maybe nobody here now to see what happen—but after accident, lots of people come from everywhere. I gonna stand here, an' when you drive, I fall off and you drive over me. How you gonna explain that, bossman?

AGENT [*frightened*]: I got nothing against you, boy. What's the matter with you? What do you want with me?

INDIAN: I want nothing from you—just to talk to me —to know who I am. Once you go into car, I am outside again. I tell you about my brother, an' how he die.

AGENT: I don't want to hear about your brother or anyone else. Now get off my car!

INDIAN: You gonna listen, mister. You gonna listen like I tell you. [*Jumps up and down on bumper.*] Boy, you ride like in bed! Mister, who am I?

AGENT: How in the devil do I know who you are—or what you want with me. I'm just doing a job—saw the burned-out camp and . . .

INDIAN: How you know who any of us are? How many of us got birth certificates to give us name and age on reserve? Maybe you think I get passport an' go to France—or marry the way bossman get married! You think that?

AGENT: I don't care who you are or what you think. Just get back to your job and leave me alone!

INDIAN [*bounces car again*]: Boy, is like pillow on

wheels! If I ever have car like this, I never walk again.

AGENT: Get off! I've got to get back into town.

INDIAN: Maybe you not go back at all.

AGENT: What do you mean by that?

INDIAN [*coming off car and walking towards* AGENT *until they are standing face to face*]: You know what it is like to kill someone—not with hate—not with any feelings here at all? [*Puts his hand over his heart.*]

AGENT [*stepping back in alarm*]: This is ridiculous! Look, boy—I'll give you anything I can, just get out of my hair. That whisky you want—I'll get it for you! Won't cost you a cent, I promise.

INDIAN: Someone that maybe you loved. Mister—I want to tell you something . . .

AGENT: No!

INDIAN [*catching hold of* AGENT's *shirt front*]: Listen, damn you! I kill like that once! You never know at Indian office—nobody tell you—nobody ever tell you! I gotta tell you about my brother—he die three, four—maybe five years ago. My friend been collecting treaty payments on his name—he know how many years now.

AGENT: You couldn't . . .

INDIAN: I couldn't?

AGENT: There are laws in this country—nobody escapes the law!

INDIAN: What law?

AGENT: The laws of the country.

INDIAN [*threateningly*]: What law?

AGENT: You mustn't kill.

INDIAN: I tell you about my brother—I tell you everything. Then you tell me if there is law for all men.

AGENT: No! Leave me alone! I don't want to hear about your brother!

INDIAN [*fiercely*]: You listen! Look around—what you see? Field an' dust, an' some work I do. You an' me—you fat, me hungry. I got nothing, an' you got money, car. Maybe you are better man than I, but I am not afraid—an' I can move faster. What happen if I get mad, an' take hammer to you?

AGENT: You . . . wouldn't . . .

INDIAN: You wrong. Nobody see us. Maybe you lucky an' get away—who believe you? You tell one story—I tell another. I lose nothing—but you gonna listen about my brother, that's for sure!

AGENT [*desperately*]: Look. boy, let's be sensible—let's behave like two grown men. I'll drive you into town—buy you a big dinner! Then we'll go out and buy that whisky I promised. You can go then, find your friends and have another party tonight. Nobody will care, and you'll have a good time!

INDIAN [*spitting*]: You lousy dog!

AGENT: Now don't get excited! I'm only saying what I think is best—if you don't want to come, then let me go and we'll forget all about today, and that we ever saw one another!

INDIAN [*releasing him*]: You think I forget I see you? I got you here like picture in my head. I try to forget you—like I try to forget my brother—but you never leave me alone!

AGENT [*trying to compose himself*]: I'm just a joe doing a job, boy—remember that. I know there's a lot bothers you—we all got problems—but take them where they belong. [*Pulls out cigarettes and nervously lights one for himself.*]

INDIAN: Gimme that!

AGENT: This is mine—I lit it for myself! Here, I'll give you another one!

INDIAN: I want that one!

AGENT: No, damn it! Have a new one.

[INDIAN *jumps behind* AGENT *and catches him with arm around throat. Then with other hand reaches out and takes lit cigarette out of* AGENT'S *mouth. Throws* AGENT *to the field.*]

AGENT [*rising and rubbing his eyes*]: What's wrong with you . . . why did you do that?

INDIAN: Get up—I want to tell you something. [AGENT *still sits, stretching and rubbing his neck.*] Get up—or I kick your brains in! [AGENT *staggers to his feet and leans uncertainly against car.*] My brother was hungry—an' he get job on farm of white boss to dig a

well. Pay is one dollar for every five feet down. My
brother dig twenty feet—two day hard work. He call up
to boss, give me planks, for the blue clay is getting wet.
To hell with what you see, boss shout down hole—just
dig. Very soon, the clay shift, an' my brother is trapped
to the shoulders. He yell, an' the water rise to his chin.
Boss, boss! He yell, pull me out! I can't move, an' the
air, she is squeezed out of me! But boss on top, he is
scared to go down in hole. He leave to go to next farm,
an' after that, another farm, until he find another Indian
to send down hole. An' all the time from down there,
my brother yell at the sky. Jesus Christ! Help me—
white man leave me here to die. But Jesus Christ not
hear my brother, an' the water she rise to his lips. Pretty
soon, he put his head back until his hair an' ears in
slimy blue clay an' water. He no more hear himself
shout—but he shout all the same!

AGENT: I wasn't there! I couldn't help him!

INDIAN: He see stars in the sky—lots of stars. A man
sees stars even in day when he look up from hole in
earth.

AGENT: I couldn't help him—I don't want to hear
about him!

INDIAN: Then Sam Cardinal come. Sam is a coward.
But when he see my brother there in well, an' the blue
clay moving around him like living thing, he go down.
Sam dig with his hands until he get rope around my
brother. Then he come up, an' he an' white bossman
pull. My brother no longer remember, an' he not hear
the angry crack of mud an' water when they pull him
free.

AGENT [*with relief*]: Then he lived! Thank God!

INDIAN: Sure he live. You hunt?

AGENT: Hunt? You mean shooting?

INDIAN: Yeh.

AGENT: Sure—I go out every year.

INDIAN: You ever shoot deer—not enough to kill,
but enough to break one leg forever? Or maybe hit deer
in eye, an' it run away, blind on one side for wolf to
kill?

AGENT: I nicked a moose two years back—never did track it down. But I didn't shoot it in the eye.

INDIAN: How you know for sure?

AGENT: Well, I just didn't. I never shoot that way.

INDIAN: You only shoot—where bullet hit you not know. Then what you do?

AGENT: I tried to track it, but there had been only a light snow, and I lost the tracks.

INDIAN: So you not follow?

AGENT: No. I walked back to camp. My friend and I had supper, and we drove home that night.

INDIAN: Forget all about moose you hurt?

AGENT: No. I did worry about what happened to him!

INDIAN: You dream of him that night?

AGENT: What the hell? Dream about a moose? There's more important things to worry about!

INDIAN: Then you not worry. You forget as soon as you can. Moose not run away from you—you run away from moose!

AGENT: I didn't . . . You're crazy! [*Moves to car but* INDIAN *jumps forward and stops him.*] Here! You leave me alone . . . you got a lot of wild talk in your head, but you can't push your weight around with me! I'm getting out of here! Hey! [INDIAN *catches him by arm and rolls him to fall face down in the dust.*]

INDIAN: What you call man who has lost his soul?

AGENT: I don't know. Let go of me!

INDIAN: We have name for man like that. You know the name?

AGENT: No, I don't. *You're breaking my arm!*

INDIAN: We call man like that sementos. Remember that name—for you are sementos.

AGENT: Please, fella—leave me alone—I never hurt you that I know of.

INDIAN: Sure. [*Releases* AGENT, *who rises to his feet, dusty and disheveled.*]

AGENT: I want to tell you something—I want you to get this straight, because every man has to make up his mind, and I've made mine up now. This has gone on far enough. If this is a joke, then I don't see the fun in it. One way or another, I'm going to get away from you, and when I do, I'm turning you in to the police! You belong in jail!

INDIAN [*laughs*]: Maybe you are man. We been in jail long time now, sementos.

AGENT: And stop calling me that name!

INDIAN: O.K., O.K.—I call you bossman. You know what bossman mean to me?

AGENT: I don't want to know.

INDIAN [*laughs again*]: You wise—you get it. I not got much to say, then you go.

AGENT [*bewildered*]: You're not going to bother me anymore?

INDIAN: I finish my story, an' you go—go to town, go to hell—go anyplace. My brother—you know what kind of life he had? He was not dead, an' he was not alive.

AGENT: You said he came out of the well safely— what are you talking about?

INDIAN: No, he was not alive. He was too near dead to live. White boss get rid of him quick. Here, says boss, here is three dollars pay. I dig twenty feet, I make four dollars, my brother say. Bossman laugh. I take dollar for shovel you leave in hole, he says. My brother come back to reserve, but he not go home. He live in my tent. At night, he wake up shouting, an' in daytime, he is like man who has no mind. He walk around, an' many times get lost in the bush, an' other Indian find him an' bring him back. He get very sick. For one month he lie in bed. Then he try to get up. But his legs an' arms are dried to the bone, like branches of dying tree.

AGENT: He must've had polio!

INDIAN: It not matter. One night, he say to me: go to other side of lake tomorrow, an' take my wife an' my son Alphonse. Take good care of 'em. I won't live the night. I reach out an' touch him, for he talk like devil fire was on him. But his head an' cheek is cold. You will live, I say to my brother, you will live, an' take care of your wife an' Alphonse yourself. But my brother shake his head. He say to me: Help me to die.

AGENT: Why . . . didn't you . . . take him to hospital?

INDIAN [*laughs bitterly*]: Hospital! A dollar he took from dying man for the shovel buried in blue clay—hospital! Burn in hell!

AGENT: No . . . no . . . this I don't understand at all.

INDIAN: I kill my brother. In my arms I hold him. He was so light—like small boy. I hold him . . . rock him back and forward like this—like mother rock us when we tiny kids. I rock him an' I cry. I get my hands tight on his neck, an' I squeeze an' I squeeze. I know he dead, an' I still squeeze an' cry, for everything is gone, an' I am old man now—only hunger an' hurt left now.

AGENT: Good God!

INDIAN: I take off his shirt an' pants—I steal everything I can wear. Then I dig under tent, where ground is soft, an' I bury my brother. After that, I go on other side of lake. When I tell my brother's wife what I did— she not say anything for long time. Then she look at me with eyes that never make tears again. Take Alphonse, she say, I go to live with every man who have me. Then she leave her tent, an' I alone with Alphonse. I take Alphonse, an' I come back. All Indians know what happen, but nobody say anything—not to me—not to you. Some halfbreed born outside reservation take my brother's name—an' you, bossman, not know.

AGENT [*quietly, as though he were the authority again*]: We have to know—you understand, don't you? You have to tell me your brother's name.

INDIAN: I know. I tell you. Was Tommy Stone.

AGENT [*takes out notebook and writes*]: Tommy Stone —good. You know what I have to do, don't you? It's my job—it's the way I feel. We all have to live within the law. Ours is a civilized country—you understand, don't you? [*Turns to car.*] I'm going now. Don't try to run before the police come.

INDIAN [*makes no attempt to hinder* AGENT]: Sure mister—you right. [AGENT *opens car door.*] Wait! I tell

you wrong! Name is not Tommy Stone—Tommy Stone
is me! Name is Johnny Stone!

AGENT [*withdraws notebook again*]: Johnny Stone?
Let's get this straight now—your brother is Johnny
Stone? And you're Tommy Stone? [INDIAN *nods.*] O.K.,
boy. I've got that. Now remember what I said, and just
stay here. [*Returns to car.*]

INDIAN: No, mister—you got whole business screwed
up again! I Johnny Stone—my brother, he is Tommy
Stone!

AGENT [*quickly getting into car and starting motor.
Rolls down window*]: Look, Indian—what in hell is
your name anyhow? Who are you?

INDIAN: My name—you want my name?
[*Either he comes out with notebook to get it, or
INDIAN suddenly opens car door and drags the
frightened AGENT out by the collar of his coat,
pushing him against the car and confronting, teas-
ing him.*]

AGENT: Yes—that's right. If it's not too much trouble to give me a straight answer. What is your name?

INDIAN: Sam Cardinal is my name.

AGENT [*with disgust*]: Now it's Sam Cardinal. What
do you take me for anyway? You waste my time—you
rough me up like I was one of your drunken Indian
friends—and now I can't get a straight answer to a simple question. But what the heck—the police can find out
who you are and what you've done.

INDIAN: No, sementos! You never find out! [*Throws
legs apart and takes a stance like man balancing on threshold.*] You go to reservation with hunder policemen. you
try to find Johnny Stone—you try find Tommy Stone—
Sam Cardinal, too—mebbe you find everybody, mebbe
you find nobody. All Indians same. Nobody. Listen to
me! One brother is dead—who? Tommy Stone? Johnny
Stone? Joe Bush? Look. [*Turns out both pockets of his
pants, holding them out, showing them empty.*] I got
nothing—nothing—no wallet—no money—no name. I
got no past . . . no future . . . nothing. I nobody. I not

even live in this world. I dead. You get it? I dead. [*Shrugs in one great gesture.*] I never been anybody. I not just dead—I never live at all. What it matter? [AGENT *has look like medieval peasant meeting leper—fear, pity, hatred.*] What it matter if I choke you till you like rag in my hands? . . . Hit you mebbe with twenty-pound hammer, break in your head like watermelon, leave you dry in wind and feed ants . . . What matter if police come an' take me? Mister! Listen, damn you—listen! One brother kill another brother—why? [*Shakes* AGENT *furiously by the lapels.*] Why? Why? Why?

> [AGENT, *suddenly really in terror, summons up initiative to get into the car and drive off.* INDIAN *just lets him go and watches him out of frame.*]

INDIAN [*quieter, asking his question of the noncountry around him*]: What anything matter? . . . Mebbe one thing matter. One brother kill another brother. Why? Is important. Why? [*Turning away. Picking up hammer.*] Ugh, sementos! [*Spits.*]

[FADE OUT.]

CHARACTERS

POP
ETHEL
GEORGE BAILEY

The scene is a farmhouse kitchen in rural Canada. It is a cluttered and inconvenient room containing a wood range, a dresser, a kitchen table, a radio and several chairs. There is a door leading to the farmyard and another to the house. A light cord, fitted with a double socket, hangs nakedly from the ceiling; a basket of unironed clothes sits under the table; an ironing board and an electric iron are in the corner and on the top of the range respectively.

As the curtain rises the radio rings with the applause of a great audience. POP, *a farmer of seventy, sitting in a kitchen armchair and wearing an ancient and battered top hat, is applauding also; on his hands he wears white cotton workman's gloves.*

RADIO VOICE: Once again our principals are led on by Mr. Panizzi . . . and they bow. You can hear the rapturous applause of this Saturday matinee audience. [*Sound of applause rises.*]

POP: Attaboy! Yippee!

RADIO VOICE: Our lovely Lucia, in her handsome green and gold first-act costume, steps forward to acknowledge a special tribute . . . [*Tremendous applause.*]

POP: Hot dog!

RADIO VOICE: And now, ladies and gentlemen, we have arrived at the first intermission in this Saturday afternoon performance of *Lucia di Lammermoor*, brought to you from the stage of the Metropolitan Opera House in New York City, and in just a few moments I shall ask the president of our Opera Radio Guild, Mrs. August Belmont, to address you.

POP: Yay, Miz' Belmont!

[ETHEL, POP's *daughter, enters; she is a hard-faced woman of forty; she takes the basket of clothes from under the table.*]

ETHEL: Poppa, turn that thing down; I can't hear myself think.

RADIO VOICE [*female*]: Friends of the Opera Guild everywhere . . .

POP: Quiet, gal; Miz' Belmont's goin' to speak.

ETHEL: I don't care who it is. You always turn it up loudest when they're clapping. My head's splitting.

POP: Leave'er be.

ETHEL: Oh, don't be so contrary! [*She turns the radio down to a murmur.*] I've got one of my sick headaches; that racket just goes through and through me like a knife. I've got ironing to do out here. [*She sets up her board from the table to a chair back, and then plugs in her iron, climbing on a chair to reach the central light socket.*]

POP: Oh no you don't. Bump, bump, bump, bump all through my op'ry. You just wait. Go lie down again. Rest your head.

ETHEL: It's got to be done. Can't wait. Plenty to do without waiting till half-past five for that row to be over.

POP: Row, eh? Say, whose house is this anyways? Mine or your'n?

ETHEL: Yours, of course, but I do the work and keep

things decent and Jim works the farm. You can't expect to have everything your own way; you know that.

POP: I'll have this my own way. Now you turn up that radio so's I can hear Miz' Belmont.

ETHEL: Oh, don't be so childish! What do you want to hear some society woman in New York for?

POP: What for? Because she's my kind, that's what for! I'm a member of the Op'ry Radio Guild; paid my three bucks and got a ticket says so. This here Miz' Belmont, she's boss of the Guild. Guess I can hear her if I want!

ETHEL: Your kind! Ptuh! [*She tests her iron by spitting on it.*]

POP: Yes, my kind and no "ptuh" about it neither. Just because you were a schoolmarm before you married a dumb farmer you think you're everybody, don't you? Well, you never had no ear for music, nor no artistic soul. You ain't never been one of the artistic crowd.

ETHEL: And you are, I suppose? [*She is now ironing as though she were punishing the clothes, sprinkling and thumping ill-naturedly.*]

POP: Durn right I am! Look at me! I'm at the op'ry, the only fella in this township that is, I betcha. And where's Jim? Layin' out in the barn asleep, though you think he's workin'. And where are you? Layin' on the bed, hatin' the world and feelin' sick, and he thinks you're workin'. You're emotionally understimulated, the both of you—

ETHEL: What did you say?

POP: You heard me good enough.

ETHEL: Listen, Poppa. I've stood a good deal from you, but I won't have that kind of talk.

POP: What's wrong with it?

ETHEL: You know, well enough. Emotion, and that. Suppose little Jimmy was to hear?

POP: Well, what if he does?

ETHEL: A child like that? Putting ideas in his head!

POP: Do him good. Any ideas he gets in this house he'll have to get from me. You and Jim ain't got none. [*He turns up the radio.*]

RADIO VOICE [*female*]: If our lives lack beauty, we are poor indeed . . .

ETHEL: Emotionally understimulated! You were always loose.

POP: Hey?

ETHEL: I know what Mother went through. [*Turns radio down.*]

POP: Oh, you do, do you? Well, you don't. Your Ma was kinda like you—just as dumb but not as mean.

ETHEL: Don't speak so of Mother!

POP: I knew your Ma better than you did. She worked like a nigger on this farm: we both did. When she wasn't workin' she was up to some religious didoes at the church. Then come forty-five or fifty she broke down and had to have a spell in the bughouse. Never properly got over it. More and more religion: more and more hell-raisin' at home. Folks say I drove her crazy. It's a lie. Emotional undernourishment is what done it, and it'll do the same for you. You an' your sick headaches!

ETHEL: Poppa, that's the meanest thing you ever said! You're a wicked old man!

POP: Yeh, but I'm happy, an' that's more than most of 'em can say 'round here. I'm the bohemian set of Smith township, all in one man. Now you let Miz' Belmont speak. [*He turns up the radio*: JIMMY's *voice, the changing voice of a boy of fourteen, is heard outside.*]

JIMMY: Hey, Maw! Hey, Maw!

RADIO VOICE: No life to-day need be starved for the fulfilment which the noblest art can give. It is to be had for the taking: great music, great drama . . .

ETHEL [*at the door, fondly*]: What is it, Lover?

JIMMY: Car comin' in from the road.

ETHEL: Do you know whose?

JIMMY: Naw: from town by the looks of it.

ETHEL: Well—don't get cold, will you, Lover? [*She closes the door and turns down radio.*]

POP: Lover! Huh!

ETHEL: Well, what about it? He's my own son, isn't he?

POP: Yeh. Bet you never called Jim "Lover."

ETHEL: Of course not. To a grown person it ain't— isn't decent.

POP: You said ain't!

ETHEL: Living with you it's a wonder any of my Normal School sticks to me at all.

POP: Never could figure why they call them things Normal. Now who's comin' here to bust in on my Saturday afternoon; the one time o' the week when I get a little food for my immortal soul.

ETHEL [*from window*]: It's that insurance agent from town.

POP: Aw, him! What's he want?

[*A loud knock at the door and* GEORGE BAILEY *enters; he is a fat man with a frequent, phlegmy laugh.*]

G.B.: Well, well, lots o' snow you got out here, eh? Afternoon, Miz' Cochran. Hi, Grandpop! Holy Gol, what are you doin' in that get-up, for Pete sake?

POP: Awright now, G.B.; awright; say your say and don't be all day over it. I'm busy.

ETHEL: Poppa, what a way to talk to a man who's just come in out of the cold. Will you have a cup of tea, Mr. Bailey?

G.B.: Sure, thanks, if you got it handy.

ETHEL: Right on the stove; always keep some going.

G.B.: Now then, Grandpop, what's the big idea? Gettin' ready for an Orange Walk, or something?

POP: If you got to know, I'm listenin' to the op'ry on the radio. I listen every Saturday afternoon. I'm a paid-up member of the Op'ry Radio Guild, same as Miz' August Belmont. This hat is what's called an op'ry hat, but I guess you wouldn't understand about that.

G.B. [*uproarious*]: Holy smoke! And what's the idea of the furnace-man's gloves?

POP: In New York white gloves for the op'ry are *dee rigger*. That's French for you can't get in without 'em.

G.B. [*choking*]: Well by gollies, now I seen everything.

POP: No you ain't: you ain't seen nothin', nor been

anywheres. That's what's wrong with you and a lot more like you. Now what do you want?

G.B.: Keep your shirt on, Grandpop. I'm here on business: 32096-B Pay Life is finished, washed up, and complete.

POP: Hey?

G.B.: Yep. Now, what d'you want to do with the money?

POP: What money?

G.B.: Your money. Your insurance policy is paid up. You were seventy a couple of days ago, weren't you?

POP: Yeh.

G.B.: Well, then— You got twelve hundred dollars comin' to you.

POP: Is that right?

G.B.: You bet it's right. Didn't you know?

POP: I'd kinda forgotten.

G.B.: Gol, you farmers! I wonder you're not all on relief, the kind of business men you are.

POP: Aw shut up. I been payin' so long I guess I forgot I was payin' for anything except to save you from honest work. Twelve hundred bucks, eh?

G.B.: A cool twelve hundred.

POP: When do I get it?

G.B.: Well, now, just a minute, now. You don't have to take the money.

POP: Oh, I don't, eh?

G.B.: No. There's a couple of options. If you want, we'll give you a hundred dollars a year in twelve equal monthly instalments, for twelve years, and if you die before it's all gone (which you will, o' course) the balance will go to your heirs, minus certain deductions for accounting and adjustment. Or if you'd rather we'll give you two hundred cash and a paid-up policy for a thousand, which would give you a smart burial and leave five or six hundred for Miz' Cochran and Jim.

ETHEL: Here's your tea.

G.B.: Yeah, thanks. [*Gulps some of it.*] What do you think he ought to do?

ETHEL: Well—it's hard to say. With twelve hundred

we could make a lot of improvements 'round the farm. I know Jim wants a tractor the worst way. But then, the thousand in the hand after Poppa's called home would certainly be welcome. Of course, we hope that won't be for many years yet.

G.B.: Nope. The old codger looks good for a while yet. Still, you know, Grandpop, at your time of life anything can happen.

POP: Yeh? Well, with all that fat on you, and that laugh you got, you might have a stroke any minute. Ever look at it that way?

G.B.: By gollies, you're a card. Ain't he a card, eh? Seventy and smart as a steel trap. A regular card.

POP: You talk like nobody ever lived to seventy before.

G.B.: The average life expectancy for men on farms is sixty-point-two years; you're living on borrowed time, Grandpop.

POP: Borrowed from who?

G.B.: What a card! Borrowed from who, he says. It's just a way of speaking; technical.

POP: Borrowed from you, I hope.

G.B.: Aw now, don't get sore. What do you want to do? Personally I'd advise the two-hundred-down-and-a-thousand-at-death plan. Nice, clean-cut proposition, and fix up for Jim and Miz' Cochran when you're gone.

POP: I ain't gone yet. I'll take the twelve hundred in cash. Got it on you?

G.B.: Eh? No. I can write you a cheque. But are you sure you want it that way?

POP: Sure I'm sure.

ETHEL: What are you up to, Poppa?

POP: None of your business.

ETHEL: He'll let you know on Monday, Mr. Bailey.

POP: I just told him. You keep out o' this.

ETHEL: Poppa and Jim and I'll talk it over to-night. We'll phone you on Monday.

POP: You and Jim nothin'. I made up my mind.

ETHEL: You haven't considered.

POP: Say, whose money is this? Ain't it my insurance?

ETHEL: Didn't you take it out to provide for your family?

POP: Damned if I remember what I took it out for after all these years. Likely I took it out because some insurance agent bamboozled me into it. Never knew it would bring me in anything.

ETHEL: Now, Poppa, you don't want to do anything foolish after all those years of paying the premium. You took out the policy to protect your family and properly speaking it's family money, and the family will decide what to do with it.

POP: What makes you so sure I'd do somethin' foolish?

ETHEL: Well, what would you do?

POP: I'd go to New York and spend it—that's what.

ETHEL: You'd what?

G.B.: Go on a tear, eh, Grandpop? By gollies you're a card!

POP: No, I ain't a card. That's what I'm goin' to do. You can write the cheque right now, and I'll catch the 9.15 into town. I got enough money to get me quite a piece of the ways without cashin' it.

G.B.: Go on! You ain't serious?

POP: Durn right I'm serious.

G.B.: You can't do that.

POP: Why not?

G.B.: Because you can't. You don't want to go to New York.

POP: Who says I don't?

G.B.: You don't know nobody there. Where'd you sleep an' eat?

POP: Hotel.

G.B.: Go on!

ETHEL: He's just keeping this up to torment me, Mr. Bailey.

POP: You keep out o' this.

G.B.: Lookit, Grandpop—are you serious?

POP: Say, how often do I have to tell you I'm serious?

G.B.: Aw, but lookit—two hundred'll buy you a nice trip if you got to go somewheres.

POP: Two hundred won't last a week where I'm goin'! Gimme the twelve hundred an' make it quick!

G.B.: Say lookit—do you know how much twelve hundred dollars is?

POP: 'Tain't much, but it'll have to do.

G.B.: Ain't much! Say lookit, do you know what's wrong with you? You're crazy, that's what! What'd you do in New York with twelve hundred dollars?

POP [*very calmly and with a full sense of the effect of what he says on* ETHEL *and* BAILEY]: I'll tell you what I'd do, since you're so nosey: I'd get some stylish clothes, and I'd go into one o' these restrunts, and I'd order vittles you never heard of—better'n the burnt truck Ethel calls food—and I'd get a bottle o' wine—cost a dollar, maybe two—and drink it all, and then I'd mosey along to the Metropolitan Opera House and I'd buy me a seat right down beside the trap-drummer, and there I'd sit an' listen, and holler and hoot and raise hell whenever I liked the music, an' throw bookies to the gals, an' wink at the chorus, and when it was over I'd go to one o' these here night-clubs an' eat some more, an' drink whisky, and watch the gals that take off their clothes—every last dud, kinda slow an' devilish till they're bare-naked—an' maybe I'd give one of 'em fifty bucks for her brazeer—

ETHEL [*scandalized*]: Poppa!

G.B.: Jeepers!

ETHEL: You carnal man!

POP: An' then I'd step along Park Avenoo, an' I'd go right up to the door, an' I'd say, "Is this where Miz' August Belmont lives?" an' the coon would say, "Yessiree!" an' I'd say, "Tell her one o' the Op'ry Guild gang from up in Canada is here, an' how'd she like to talk over things—"

G.B.: Say listen, Grandpop: you're nuts.

ETHEL: He must be. Mother was like that at the last, you know.

POP: She was not: your Ma used to think the Baptist preacher was chasin' her to cut the buttons off her boots, but that was as far as she got. She never had the gumption to pump up a real good dream. Emotional under-nourishment: that was what ailed your Ma.

ETHEL: There you go again! He's been talking that indecent stuff all afternoon.

POP: 'Tain't indecent. It's the truth. No food for your immortal souls—that's what ails everybody 'round here —little, shriveled-up, peanut-size souls. [*He turns up the radio with a jerk.*]

RADIO VOICE [*blaring*]: . . . render life gracious with the boon of art . . .

ETHEL [*turning radio down*]: Is that what your soul feeds on? Restrunts with shameless women in 'em?

POP: Yeah, an' music an' booze an' good food an' high-toned conversation—all the things a man can't get here because everybody's too damn dumb to know they're alive. Why do you think so many people go to the bughouse around here. anyways? Because they've starved an' tormented their souls, that's why! Because they're against God an' don't know it, that's why!

ETHEL: That's blasphemous!

POP: It ain't blasphemous! They try to make God in their own little image an' they can't do it same as you can't catch Niagara Falls in a teacup. God likes music an' naked women an' I'm happy to follow his example.

ETHEL [*shrieks in outrage*]: Eeeeeek!

G.B. [*on firm moral ground at last*]: That'll do now! That'll just do o' that! I ain't goin' to listen to no such smut: I got a kiddy at home not three yet! Do you think I'm goin' to give you twelve hundred dollars for that kind o' thing? It wouldn't be business ethics! Say, you better look out I don't report this to the Ministerial Alliance! They'd tell you where you got off, darn soon!

POP: You mean you won't give me the money?

G.B.: Naw!

POP: You want me to have to write to head office an' ask why?

G.B.: I'll tell 'em. Unsound mind, that's why.

POP: What's your proof?

G.B.: You just say what you said about God to any doctor, that's all.

POP: Yeah, but if I don't?

G.B.: Well—

POP: You'd look kinda silly, wouldn't you?

G.B.: Now lookit—

POP: Would it cost you the agency, do you think?

G.B.: Aw, now lookit here—

POP: A libel suit'd come pretty dear to your company, anyways.

G.B.: Libel?

POP: Libellous to say a man's crazy.

G.B.: Miz' Cochran would back me up.

POP: Serious thing, tryin' to put a man in the bughouse just when he gets some money. Look bad in court.

G.B. [*deflated*]: Aw, have it your own way. I'll write you a cheque.

[*He sits at the table and does so.*]

POP: Make it nice an' plain, now. [*He turns up the radio.*]

RADIO VOICE [*male, again*]: You have been listening to Mrs. August Belmont, president of the Metropolitan Opera Guild, in one of the series of intermission talks which is a regular feature of this Saturday afternoon broadcast. And now to give you a brief outline of Act II of Gaetano Donizetti's romantic masterwork, *Lucia di Lammermoor*: the curtain rises to disclose the magnificent hall of Sir Henry Ashton's castle. Norman (played this afternoon by the American baritone Elmer Backhouse) tells Sir Henry (Mr. Dudelsack) that he need have no fear that Lucy will offer opposition to the proposed marriage with Lord Arthur Bucklaw (played this afternoon by Listino di Prezzi) as her letters to Edgar (Mr. Posaun in to-day's performance) have been intercepted and forgeries substituted for them which will leave no doubt of his faithlessness. At this point Lucia (Miss Fognatura) enters (in a gown of greenish-blue taffeta relieved by cerise gussets and a fichu) to a delicately orchestrated passage for wind and strings. Then, supported entirely by wind, Lucy tells her brother that her hand is promised to another, whereupon he produces the forged letters. "The papers," she cries: "La lettera, mio Dio!" whereupon follows a lively upward rush of brass . . .

G.B. [*during the foregoing*]: Here. Well, g'day, Miz' Cochran. [*He listens to the radio ecstasies.*] Cheest! [*He goes out.*]

ETHEL [*turning the radio down*]: Well?

POP: Yeah?

ETHEL: When you've squandered the money—what then?

POP: I'll be back. This is my farm, remember. I'll have some stories to tell you, Ethel. Maybe that Home an' School Club o' yours'll ask me to address 'em on my experiences. I'll show 'em the programs from the op'ry —maybe even let 'em see my fifty-buck brazeer. [*A pause.*]

ETHEL [*sitting down*]: Listen, Poppa; you haven't thought about this.

POP: Are we goin' to go through all that again?

ETHEL: Yes. You know what people will say when you come back. They'll say a fool and his money are soon parted. They'll say there's no fool like an old fool.

POP: What do I care what they say?

ETHEL: This dream of yours is crazy, like Mr. Bailey says. If you go to New York you'll just be a lost old man, and everybody will laugh at you and rob you.

POP: How do you know?

ETHEL: I know. You don't belong there. You belong right here in this township, though you've been ungrateful and abused it, just because it isn't full of opera and restrunts and hussies. This township's been good to you— given you a good living—

POP: You mean I've been able to work like an ox here and keep the sheriff the other side o' the gate?

ETHEL: That's more than many people have had.

POP: Well 'tain't enough for me. What about my soul? What's this township ever give me for that, eh? There was just one purty thing in sight o' this farm—row of elms along the road; they cut down the elms to widen the road an' then never widened it.

ETHEL: You talk about your soul in a way that makes me blush. Soul to you just means the pleasures of the flesh. We got a fine church, with almost half the debt paid off on it—

POP: Yeah, an' your Ma pretty near bled me white over that debt. Last fifty bucks I gave 'em was for a bell, and what'd they do? Bought a new stove with it.

ETHEL: They needed a stove.

POP: Yeah, an' they needed a bell. But that's always the way around here; necessities first, every time.

ETHEL: And what's wrong with that?

POP: Because there's always a gol-danged necessity to get in the way whenever you want somethin' purty. There's always somebody starvin', or a sewer needs diggin', or some damn necessary nuisance to hog all your time an' energy an' money if you go lookin' for it. Somebody's got to take the bull by the horns an' ignore the necessities if we're ever goin' to have any o' the things that make life worth livin'.

ETHEL: What makes life worth living? You seem to think nothing is worth having but a high old time. Don't you ever think of duty?

POP: I've had a bellyful o' duty. I've got somethin' in me that wants more than duty an' work.

ETHEL: Yes, and you've told me what it is. Rich food and alcohol and lewd women. A fine thing, at your age!

POP: Aw—that's just a way of speakin'. I want what's warm an'—kind of mysterious; somethin' to make you laugh an' talk big, an'—oh, you wouldn't know. You just sit there, lookin' like a meat-axe, an' won't even try to see what I'm drivin' at. Say listen, Ethel: what d'you get out o' life anyways?

ETHEL: Well, that's a fine question!

POP: Now don't get mean about it. You called my New York trip a dream; what's your dream?

ETHEL: I'm not the dreaming kind.

POP: Oh yes you are. You cranky ones, you're the

ones with dreams, all right. What do you think o' your-self, Ethel?

ETHEL: Well— [*Pause.*] I think I'm a dutiful wom-an.

POP: A good woman?

ETHEL [*overcoming her aversion to the luxury of di-rect self-praise*]: Yes.

POP: And is that what you want out o' life?

ETHEL: It's my reward for a lot of work and self-de-nial.

POP: Go on.

ETHEL: You talk about dreams. Why do you think I live the way I do? Because it's right, first of all. And there are rewards on earth, too. When I walk into church or a meeting I know what people say: they say, "There's Ethel Cochran; she stands on her own two feet, and never asks anything from anybody; she has a hard enough row to hoe, too, but you never hear a peep out of her."

POP: An' you like that, eh? Kind o' strong-woman stuff?

ETHEL: I'm glad I'm well-thought-of. "You never see *her* wash out after Monday noon," they say.

POP: And that's what you want in life? To be a wom-an that nobody can help or give anything to? Come on, Ethel; what else?

ETHEL: Well—you wouldn't understand.

POP: I'm trying. Go on.

ETHEL: I want to be remembered.

POP: Yeah? How?

ETHEL: You're not going to New York, are you?

POP: Who says I ain't?

ETHEL: Then let's not go on talking.

POP: Now Ethel, we ain't goin' to stop. I want to know what goes on inside you. Get yourself a cup o' tea, and give me one too an' let's have this out. [ETHEL *goes to get the tea.*] I think I see what you're up to. You don't want me to go to New York because you want that money for somethin' else. Is that it?

ETHEL: Here's your tea.

POP: Sit down.

ETHEL: Rather stand.

POP: Now what is it you want? Not a tractor, I bet. Come on, now. Is it something for Lover? You want to send him to college, maybe?

ETHEL: Naturally I want to see Jimmy get a good start in life. I—I've done a little saving toward it.

POP: Yeah, I know. Cheatin' on me an' Jim. I know where you got it hid, too. But that ain't it. I can tell.

ETHEL: Of course you'd make it sound ugly. I'm determined that my boy shall be a pharmacist, and I've had to find my own way of financing it.

POP: But that ain't your real ambition. Come on, Ethel.

ETHEL: No.

POP: Unless you tell me, I'm certain to go on my trip and spend all the money, and bang goes your dream. But if you tell me, you've got a chance. It's up to you. [*Pours his tea in his saucer and drinks noisily.*]

ETHEL: That'd look fine in a New York restrunt. What would the brazen women say?

POP: They'd put up with it long's I had a dollar. Don't stall, Ethel. We got nearest to your dream when you said you wanted to be remembered. Come on, now.

ETHEL: I won't tell you.

POP: Don't, then. [*Rises purposefully.*] Got a clean shirt for me? I'll be getting ready to go.

ETHEL [*wavers for a moment, then breaks into painful, ugly tears*]: Poppa!

POP: Yeah?

ETHEL: I want—a headstone.

POP: You want a what?

ETHEL: A headstone. A granite one.

POP [*sits, flabbergasted*]: Well good God Almighty!

ETHEL [*weeping freely now*]: Mother's grave just has a plain marker. But it's in a wonderful position. Soon all the land around it will be sold off and who can tell where we'll be buried? Higgledy-piggledy all over the place, most likely. We ought to have a proper family plot, with a chain fence round it, and a headstone with the family name on it. A headstone! Oh, a big family headstone! We could get that plot surrounding Mother, right on the crest of the hill, and it'd be seen from every place in the cemetery. A headstone! Not a broken pillar, or a draped urn, or anything flashy and cheap, but a great big block of granite—the gray, not the red—smooth-finished on the faces, but rough on the sides and top, and the name on the base, cut deep! Dignified! Quiet! But the best quality—the finest in the cemetery. I want it! I want it! Then Mother and I, and Lover and Jim and you could all be there together at last—

POP: Envied by every stiff in the township!

ETHEL: I want it! I want it!

POP: I can see that.

ETHEL: Not even a text. No "Rest in the Lord" or "Till The Day Break" or anything. Just the name.

POP: And that's what you want more than anything else?

ETHEL: Yes. You had to know. Now you know. Jim doesn't care about—well, about nice things like that. And of course it isn't his name.

POP: And when Bailey came in here with twelve hundred bucks for me you seen your gravestone as good as raised?

ETHEL: Yes.

POP: Pretty vain idea, ain't it?

ETHEL: No it ain't—isn't. We've been something in this township. You would never run for council, though you could have been reeve if you'd tried. But Mother was a real figure here, especially the four or five years before—she had to go to That Place. And I've tried to follow where she went. She deserves something, and so do I. Missions, Temperance, the W.A.—we've done our share and more. And when we're gone we deserve something that'll last. That money would cover it all, and leave a little something to provide for Perpetual Care. It's not vain to want your due.

POP: Don't follow your Ma's trail as far as the bughouse, Ethel. It's cost a darn sight more than my insurance money to keep you there.

ETHEL: It was silly of me to tell you. You've got no feeling for anything that really matters. I've just put a stick in your hand to beat me with.

POP: Drink your tea an' blow your nose an' shut up. Ain't there a pen-an'-ink someplace here? [*He searches in the dresser drawers.*] Yeah, here she is. Y'know, I never could play no instrument nor draw worth a cent, but before my fingers got so stiff I was a real pretty writer. Your Ma once got me to write out a presentation address to a preacher that was leavin', and when it was done it just looked like a page o' copperplate. There, Ethel; there's your cheque, endorsed and made over to you.

[ETHEL *takes the cheque, amazed.*]

ETHEL: Poppa!

POP: Buy yourself a nice tombstone. [*He sits.*] Y'know, when you was a little thing, you was as pretty as all-get-out, and till you got to be about fourteen you meant more to me than anything else on God's earth. But then you got religion, and began to favor your Ma, and I guess it was as if you'd died to me, and everything I liked. So far as I'm concerned, this here tombstone's mostly for the little one I lost.

ETHEL: Poppa, we've had our disagreements, but that's past. It'll be different now. [*She has put the cheque in her pocket, changed her mind, and tucked it in her bosom.*]

POP: Because I bought you a tombstone? Naw. You've changed, Ethel, and you've been what you are more than twice as long as you were my child.

ETHEL: But I don't understand. You do this wonderful, generous thing, and yet you seem so bitter. I know you haven't much feeling for me.

POP: Oh, yes I have; I pity you twelve hundred bucks' worth an' maybe more.

ETHEL: But why—?

POP: Aw, never mind. Ethel, you've got the power of goodness.

ETHEL [*modest*]: Oh, Poppa!

POP: Don't take it as a compliment. There's a special

kind o' power that comes from the belief that you're
right. Whether you really are right or not doesn't matter: it's the belief that counts. Your belief in your own
goodness makes you awful strong, Ethel, and you've
kind of overlaid me with it. I can't stand up to it.

ETHEL: I don't know what you're talking about. I
don't know what to say about this, Poppa. There must
be depths of good in you I never suspected. It just goes
to show that we shouldn't judge.

JIMMY'S VOICE [*outside*]: Hey, Maw!

POP: There's your future druggist hollerin'.

ETHEL [*at the door, her voice trilling with happiness*]:
Yes, Lover?

JIMMY'S VOICE: How long till supper, Maw?

ETHEL: Oh, you greedy thing! More'n an hour. D'you
want me to fix you a piece?

JIMMY'S VOICE: Naw, I'll wait.

ETHEL: I'm going to open a jar of maple surp. Pan-
cakes, Lover!

[*She closes the door.*]

POP: Lover! Emotional understimulation!

[ETHEL *comes behind him and gives him a dry,
shy kiss on the brow. Then she goes to the radio
and turns it on, with an indulgent smile toward
him. It hums a little as it warms.*]

POP: Naw. Turn it off. Don't want it now. I been
overlaid and I got to get myself back in shape. Maybe I
been emotionally overstimulated. But I ain't overlaid for
good, Ethel, an' that stone'll rest lighter on me than it
will on you.

[*During this speech* ETHEL *has been getting flour,
bowls and other supplies out of the dresser, with
her back to* POP. *He has fished a long pair of black
stockings out of the clothesbasket and wrapped
them around his arm like a mourner's crêpe; he
now tilts back in his chair and surveys* ETHEL's
back quizzically, whistling an air from Lucia,
which mingles with the sound of ETHEL's *eggbeater
as the curtain falls.*]

Protest

NORMAN WILLIAMS

THE CHARACTERS

THE GRANDMOTHER
THE MOTHER
THE FATHER
THE DAUGHTER

The time is 1900.

The setting is the main room of a Japanese home. It is bright and airy with walls consisting of light-coloured wooden panels. There are entrances at left, at right, and at centre back. In the back wall, left of centre, is a gilded Buddhist shrine. To the right and down-stage are the low black tables and cushions which represent the dining furniture of the Japanese household. To the left and looking incongruously out of place is the only piece of Western furniture in the room, a plain wooden chair. At front, left, are two floor cushions.

The stage is momentarily empty. Then, from centre back, the GRANDMOTHER *enters. She is a tiny, dignified lady of advanced years. She carries a bowl and crosses the room to add it to those already on the tables. As she bends to do so, she catches sight of the chair, left, drops the dish with a crash and retreats with a shrill shriek towards centre back.*

GRANDMOTHER [*calling*]: Daughter! Daughter! Come here! Come here!

MOTHER [*enters hurriedly from the back*]: What's the matter? What is it?

GRANDMOTHER [*clutches her and points to the chair*]: That? What is that?

MOTHER [*detaches herself and goes gingerly towards the chair*]: I'm—not sure. I've never seen one before—

GRANDMOTHER [*shrieks*]: Don't go too close! Be careful. Be careful!

MOTHER: It's all right, Mother. [*She moves closer.*]

GRANDMOTHER: Oh, the merciful Buddha protect you.

MOTHER [*curious*]: I *believe* I know what it is. [*She is very close to it now. The* GRANDMOTHER *is trembling and close to sobbing.*]

GRANDMOTHER: Oh, take care. Take care!

MOTHER [*bending low and peering under the chair*]: Yes, I'm sure. It's a chair.

GRANDMOTHER: What is—a—chair? What is it for?

MOTHER: To sit on. I've heard them described.

GRANDMOTHER: To sit on? What kind of beast would seat itself on a hideous thing like that?

MOTHER: Men, Mother; men sit on them.

GRANDMOTHER: I don't believe it. Only evil spirits would sit on a devilish device like that. [*The* MOTHER *puts out her hand to touch it.*] Don't touch it. Oh, don't touch it!

MOTHER [*drawing back; a trifle nervously*]: It's only made of wood.

GRANDMOTHER: Evil and sorcery reside in wood as well as in anything else.

> [*Enter the* FATHER *from right. The* MOTHER *and* GRANDMOTHER *return his bow.*]

FATHER: Did I hear someone shriek? I wasn't properly dressed or I would have come before now to see what the trouble was.

GRANDMOTHER: I shrieked! There are devils in the house, and we are all at the mercy of evil!

FATHER: What's this, my esteemed mother? Devils? Evil?

GRANDMOTHER: There! [*She points an accusing finger at the chair.*]

FATHER: A chair.

MOTHER: I *told* you it was a chair.

FATHER: Where did it come from?

MOTHER: We don't know. It wasn't here a short time ago; I have been in and out putting the bowls on the table.

FATHER [*crosses to it, wonderingly*]: A chair. In our house.

MOTHER: You have seen one before, my husband?

FATHER: I have seen them in Tokyo.

MOTHER: Are they made in Tokyo?

FATHER [*laughs*]: No, they come from the Western countries. The Western barbarians sit on them all the time.

GRANDMOTHER: Didn't I say they were from the devil?

FATHER: Here is how they do it. [*He is about to sit in the chair as the* GRANDMOTHER, *as if pursued by seven devils, runs wailing out of the room, centre back.*]

MOTHER: Oh, you have really frightened her now.

FATHER [*seriously*]: That was wickedly unfilial of me. I apologize. [*He bows.*]

MOTHER [*lowering her eyes*]: I should not have pointed out that you had.

FATHER: You were quite correct. It is right for you to point out my blunders. You know I have always been liberal in matters such as that.

[*A sound of sobbing is heard, off.*]

MOTHER: I'm afraid your poor mother is crying with fright.

FATHER: I will reassure her. [*Secretly, with mischief.*] But, just before I do, here is how they do it! [*He lets his seat rest for just a few moments on the chair and then jumps up. But the sight of him even that briefly in this unaccustomed posture is too much for the*

MOTHER. *She bursts into laughter as he crosses to centre back.*]

MOTHER: You look like a duck.

FATHER [*calling softly*]: Mother. [*The sobbing, off, hesitates, ceases. Calls again.*] Mother, your unworthy son is calling you.

GRANDMOTHER [*off*]: What is it, my revered son?

FATHER: I send my humble respects to my aged mother and apologize in the dust for frightening her.

GRANDMOTHER: You are—a good son, and I know you wouldn't frighten me purposely.

FATHER: Will you return to us now?

GRANDMOTHER: Are you sitting on—"It"?

FATHER: No, my mother.

GRANDMOTHER: Are you going to sit on it?

FATHER: No, my mother.

GRANDMOTHER: Are you touching it?

FATHER: No.

GRANDMOTHER: Are you going to touch it?

FATHER: No.

GRANDMOTHER: Has it been removed from the room?

FATHER: No.

GRANDMOTHER: It is not a good influence in the room. It should be removed.

FATHER: Do you want me to touch it?

GRANDMOTHER: No! No! Don't touch it!

FATHER: Then how am I to remove it, revered Mother?

[*The* GRANDMOTHER *appears up-stage.*]

GRANDMOTHER: If we pray to the Buddha, he will remove it.

FATHER: I wish I knew how it got here.

MOTHER: It must *belong* to someone.

FATHER: But to whom?

[*At this, the* DAUGHTER, *a lovely, proud-looking girl of seventeen, enters quickly from left. She stands facing them.*]

DAUGHTER [*defiantly*]: It is mine!

FATHER: }
MOTHER: } Yours!

GRANDMOTHER [*crossing towards her but wary of the chair*]: Yours? It was you who brought this sorcerer's instrument into the home of your parents? You who set it down before the shrine of the sacred Buddha?

DAUGHTER [*calmly*]: Yes, it was.

GRANDMOTHER [*stretching out her arms to the Buddha*]: Have compassion on the house where evil enters in the hands of its only daughter.

MOTHER: How could you do such a thing? Aren't you ashamed?

FATHER [*quietly*]: Revered Mother, will you please your son by going to your room to prepare for the evening meal?

GRANDMOTHER [*dropping her arms, looking old and weary*]: I will go.

[*She moves slowly across and out, right. The* MOTHER *and* FATHER *bow to her.*]

MOTHER: Yes, honoured Mother-in-law, go and prepare for your evening meal, and we will take care of this affair.

FATHER: And, my wife, if we are to have supper someone must be in the kitchen to prepare it.

MOTHER: That is so. [*She bows submissively and exits up-stage.*]

[*The* FATHER *walks to the chair and sits down. The* DAUGHTER *stands unmoving in her original position.*]

FATHER: It's not a very comfortable chair, is it?

DAUGHTER: *We* aren't used to sitting in chairs.

FATHER: That is true. Still, I have done so before. [*The* DAUGHTER *shows interest.*] In the big cities they are quite commonly seen. But they aren't plain wooden ones like this. Some of them I have seen are made of shining brown cow-hide; cool to the touch and so slippery I would be afraid to sit in one. Others are huge affairs with springs in the seat, and when you sit down it would seem you are sinking into a deep, soft cloud. I imagine the Westerners use them for sleeping. At least the ones I saw seated in them seemed on the verge of sleep.

DAUGHTER: Oh, there are so many things I have *never* seen.

FATHER: That is true of most of us, and many of the things we never see are right before our eyes all the time.

DAUGHTER: I didn't mean *those* things. I mean the new, wonderful things the Westerners have.

FATHER [*rises and takes the chair out, left*]: I will put this into the "shoe-off" room; it disturbs your grandmother.

DAUGHTER: And may I keep it in my room?

FATHER: We will have to think about that.

DAUGHTER: Ishimoto said it was a very fine chair and that houses in America have twenty or thirty each in them.

FATHER [*returns from left*]: So it was Ishimoto who gave you the chair? I guessed it was.

DAUGHTER: He didn't give it to me. I bought it.

FATHER: How could you buy it? You have no money. [*The* FATHER *seats himself on one of the cushions, left.*]

DAUGHTER: I paid him with two of my pearl haircombs, my writing brush, and the red sash I had at the New Year.

FATHER: And that is how Ishimoto grows richer day by day. Sit here opposite me, and let us talk together as we used to when you were a child. [*The* DAUGHTER *seats herself on the cushion opposite him.*] It is here, on this very spot, your old teacher used to teach you your lessons. Don't you remember any longer, with any fondness, all that he told you of our Japanese past, our culture and our wise men, our traditions, and the courageous lives of our history's heroines?

DAUGHTER: I only remember one thing about those lessons, my father.

FATHER: And what is that?

DAUGHTER: That all the two hours my old teacher sat where you sit now and droned into my ear our Japanese past, I was made to sit motionless, so. [*She assumes the rigid posture of the Japanese student.*] Never once was I allowed to move an arm, a hand, or my littlest finger. How the minutes dragged on! I thought he would never finish, that I would turn to stone on the spot and never be able to move again, or run and play in the courtyard.

FATHER: It is true the discipline was harsh—

DAUGHTER: One day, I remember, I felt my left foot grow numb and I ventured to move my trunk the tiniest fraction to relieve the pressure on it. My teacher saw me; he gave me a look like the black God of War. Without a word to me, he stopped the lesson; he got up and left without a bow. I could hear him in the next room complaining loudly to you and saying how unworthy I was. I was left crying with fear and shame.

FATHER: I remember.

DAUGHTER: From that day on, I had my lessons from him in the outer room with no heat, although it was December and the snow was piled high in the streets. I would turn purple with the cold, but dared not shiver or tremble in the slightest.

FATHER: Yes, yes. Your mother and I discussed it through an entire night.

DAUGHTER: I didn't know you noticed . . . or cared.

FATHER: We did. We were afraid it would be too hard on you but we decided, in the dawn light, rightly or wrongly, that discipline was the path to wisdom and virtue. We wanted our daughter to be wise and virtuous. We followed custom.

DAUGHTER: Custom!

FATHER: I know you think custom ancient and barbaric.

DAUGHTER: Yes, I do.

FATHER: Yet it is not. It does not diminish men's actions. It gives those actions form. It is our way of respecting others.

DAUGHTER: But it never changes. [*Proudly.*] This is the year 1900, you know.

FATHER [*amused*]: A Western year. 1900, eh? Did Mr. Ishimoto give you that information? Perhaps free, with the chair?

DAUGHTER [*with child-like mysteriousness*]: Oh, I had heard what year it was.

FATHER: Will you believe me if I tell you something?

DAUGHTER: I will try.

FATHER: It is not true that custom fails to change.

DAUGHTER: I don't see that it does.

FATHER: You have not observed it long enough. Do you know there was a day when meat was never eaten in this house? To eat meat was looked upon as a loathsome evil because the Buddha himself forbade the killing of animals. But gradually the belief began to change. Little by little we were invaded by new ideas from the Western world. I well remember the day I first ordered the preparation of meat in this house. My honoured mother spent that day in her room at her personal shrine praying for all of us who dared to break a tradition over a thousand years old. She ate nothing for three days and for two years and more would not eat with us in this room or go near the kitchen where the meat was prepared. To this very hour she has never tasted it and will not if she lives another hundred years.

DAUGHTER: She is stubborn.

FATHER: We must all be stubborn in what we believe or one day find we believe in nothing.

DAUGHTER: But you said you change your beliefs.

FATHER: I do, and have, and will. When others began to eat meat, I said to myself: Is there some good in this? And I inquired and found there was; that animal flesh makes men stronger and builds muscles to withstand cold and hard work. And so I said, "I will change. We will eat meat in my house." And we did. But not until I had considered it carefully and weighed the custom against the new belief.

DAUGHTER: Perhaps you have changed—in small things.

FATHER: Small things?

DAUGHTER: Eating meat is a small thing to me when I see how chained our lives are.

FATHER: We are not chained. We are civilized and reserved, it is true—

DAUGHTER: You call it civilized and reserved, but I call it a prison. I am in a prison and I yearn to be free.

[*Enter* MOTHER *at centre back. She carries a bowl, crosses to the table and places the bowl on it. She putters about as an excuse for eavesdropping.*]

FATHER: Free to do as you please?

DAUGHTER: Free to do as—

FATHER: As—what?

DAUGHTER: As other women do.

FATHER: What other women?

DAUGHTER: Western women.

FATHER: Ishimoto!

DAUGHTER: Mr. Ishimoto has told me many things; he has painted me a picture of another world—a world I long to know and be a part of. In that world, women are free to grow and blossom instead of sitting with folded hands and allowing life to slip away from them as they do here.

FATHER: Women here live honourable lives.

DAUGHTER [*flatly*]: They obey their husbands and bear children and die with never a question on their lips.

FATHER: Is that not honourable?

DAUGHTER: It is not freedom. In the Western lands women do not hide behind shutters and sit in an eternal twilight while others regulate their lives.

FATHER: They do not?

DAUGHTER: No. There they walk freely on the streets or go into tea-houses alone and order what they wish and pay for it themselves, for they have their own money.

FATHER: I have heard of that.

DAUGHTER: But, most important, they go to school and learn what men learn. They talk to men as their equals and, Mr. Ishimoto says, a wife may even criticize her husband.

[*The* MOTHER, *who has listened in growing horror, utters an exclamation at this and hurriedly leaves the room.*]

FATHER: My daughter—

DAUGHTER: And it is said that men embrace their

wives in front of others and show affection in ways I don't properly understand. But I know it is by more than a bow.

FATHER: It is. I have heard of it. It is called kissing.

DAUGHTER: That's it. That is what Mr. Ishimoto called it.

FATHER: But a kiss is only another custom, strange to us but familiar to them. There is as much feeling of the heart in a bow as there is in a kiss. And yet, to my mind, a bow is in good form because it is an unselfish recognition of another; while a kiss, which is part of love-making, shows a desire for one's own pleasure.

DAUGHTER: It sounds exciting and natural to me.

FATHER: What is natural and what is not? It would seem that all of life must be regulated in some way if we are to live together. One could argue that it is "natural" to have customs to regulate "naturalness."

DAUGHTER [*boldly, then hesitatingly*]: I think it is natural for—

FATHER: For what?

DAUGHTER: For a girl to choose her own husband.

FATHER [*rises*]: What do you say? Oh, this is too much. I have sat here patiently trying to reason with you, but this is too much.

DAUGHTER: I don't want to marry a man I've never seen.

FATHER: Ungrateful, unfilial child! What do you know, what does any young girl know about choosing a husband? What can she know of his means, his family, his character, his education, which are what matter in a husband?

DAUGHTER: I *won't!* I *won't* marry him.

FATHER: I draw the line. Finally and firmly. Have all the romantic day-dreams you like—no doubt your husband will pay for them—but you *will* marry the man we have chosen for you.

DAUGHTER [*beating her hands on the floor*]: No, no, no, no.

FATHER: This is my fault. I should have supervised your education.

DAUGHTER [*sobbing*]: Education.

FATHER: But the education of a daughter is always in the hands of the women of the house.

DAUGHTER [*triumphantly*]: There, you see? Another *custom!*

[*Enter the* MOTHER, *who brings more bowls to the table. She arranges the cushions and exits right.*]

FATHER: Come. Pick yourself up. Our meal is ready.

[*The* DAUGHTER *rises and wipes her eyes on her sleeve.*

[*The* FATHER *takes up a position before the gilded shrine.*

[*Enter* MOTHER *and* GRANDMOTHER *from right. They cross and take up positions behind the* FA-THER. *The* DAUGHTER *occupies the final position. At last they are in a row the shape of a semicircle.*]

FATHER: Lord Buddha, Light of Heaven and Earth, giver of Eternal Life, all-wise and merciful, look upon your humble servants and receive their gratitude for your compassionate gift of food. [*He bows low to the shrine and moves to the right towards the table.*

[*The* GRANDMOTHER *then bows a deep and reverent bow, going down on her knees to do so. The* MOTHER *bows deeply from the waist. They move away to the right.*

[*The* DAUGHTER *gives a brief and perfunctory bow and joins the rest.*

[*They seat themselves at the table, the* FATHER *first in accordance with precedence, and begin their meal. There is silence for several moments.*]

DAUGHTER: Father!

FATHER:
MOTHER: } Shhhhhhh!
GRANDMOTHER:

[*Silence for a few moments.*]

DAUGHTER [*puts down her bowl, in suppressed emotion*]: I can't—

GRANDMOTHER [*flatly*]: It is not proper to speak at meals.

[*There is silence again as the* DAUGHTER *fidgets and frets, growing more despairing as the silent moments pass.*]

MOTHER [*in a whisper*]: Don't fidget, daughter. You are disturbing everyone. Calm and tranquillity at mealtime—

DAUGHTER: Oh, none of you care, none of you care. My heart could be breaking and you would sit there eating silently like cows because it is the custom. [*She rises quickly.*]

MOTHER: Daughter! What are you doing?

GRANDMOTHER: The sacred Buddha protect us! She has risen from the table.

MOTHER: Child, child, think what you are doing. No woman rises from her cushion before the master of the household and then only when all are finished. It is an iron rule.

FATHER: I rise, too. [*Bows to the* GRANDMOTHER *and* MOTHER.] I beg your forgiveness. [*They return his bow. He gets up and goes towards the* DAUGHTER.] Are you completely mad? Have you no respect left at all for your revered mother and your honoured grandmother? Remember, your ideas aren't the only ideas in the world, and while you are in your father's house—

DAUGHTER: [*interrupting*]: How long will I *be* in it?

GRANDMOTHER: } [*in horror*] She has interrupted him.
MOTHER:

[*They hide their faces.*]

DAUGHTER: In a year, a little year, I shall go to some strange house and sit upon the bridal couch with downcast eyes, waiting for a stranger to come and claim me for his slave. I will *not* do it. I will not. I will show you. [*She runs quickly away and out, left.*]

FATHER [*turns back to the table and bows again to the two women*]: We shall continue our meal. [*He sits and they eat silently.*

[*After a few moments there is a sound of sobbing off, left. Those at the table give no indication they hear.*

[*Enter,* DAUGHTER *from left, much transformed and near to hysteria. She has let down her sleek, black hair from its coils and has cut it down to short and jagged lengths. Her gown is covered with hair and she is cutting what lengths remain as she enters.*]

DAUGHTER: There! Now he will not marry me, whoever he is.

[*The three at the table have, in spite of their control, looked at the* DAUGHTER *and a kind of paralysis has overcome them at the shocking sight. The* FATHER *has half risen, the* GRANDMOTHER *has hidden her face, the* MOTHER's *hands are held up as if to ward off a blow.*

FATHER [*bows hastily to the* MOTHER *and* GRANDMOTHER]: I must rise. [*They bow to him. He rises and faces the* DAUGHTER.]

DAUGHTER [*in her sobs*]: You see, I meant what I said.

FATHER: You have cut your hair! As a widow would do.

DAUGHTER: Yes, like a widow.

FATHER: This is madness.

DAUGHTER: And if it grows in before my wedding day, I shall pull it out by the roots.

FATHER: Wicked child.

DAUGHTER: No superstitious man would marry me now, looking like a widow, for fear he would die. And they are all superstitious and—stupid.

[*She exits left. The* GRANDMOTHER *has risen, shaking and trembling, from her cushion. She makes her way across the room to the shrine in the desperate, plodding fashion of a wanderer athirst in the desert who sights an oasis.*]

GRANDMOTHER: I must regain my tranquillity. [*She kneels before the Buddha and is motionless during the following.*]

MOTHER [*still seated*]: My husband!

FATHER: Yes.

MOTHER: Is this—my fault? Some fault of mine?

FATHER: No, it is mine. How could you know of all

the new ideas abroad in our country or how they might change your daughter from day to day, tearing her from the old ways?

MOTHER: If she does not marry him, there will be great shame on our family name.

FATHER: It will be remembered from generation to generation.

MOTHER: Could she not be forced to marry him?

FATHER: She could be.

[*The* GRANDMOTHER *rises and comes to them.*]

GRANDMOTHER: She is not a child to be forced. She would only grow more rebellious and by her unwifely actions bring shame to our good name after her marriage.

MOTHER: What are we to do?

GRANDMOTHER [*despairingly*]: Oh, the old, safe ways are crumbling. In my day, tradition and discipline gave women strength in their duty and joy in their lives. But now, the scourge has spread across the land, destroying the ancient virtues of humility and modesty. Have you not seen, even here, how some women hurry along the paths at an unseemly rate until they are walking like men?

MOTHER: I have seen that.

GRANDMOTHER: They no longer arrange flowers in the classical manner but place them in the vase as if they were growing in natural chaos.

FATHER: It is so.

GRANDMOTHER: They neglect to subdue their voices when they speak and fail to bow to their elders at the proper times—oh, it is all around us—all around us—and now it has struck our home.

FATHER: It is my fault. Not to have protected her from these influences was a great fault in me.

GRANDMOTHER: Forgive my rude contradiction, but the fault is ours.

MOTHER: Yes, it is ours. In our hands she was moulded.

GRANDMOTHER: More particularly, the fault is mine.

As the eldest, it was my duty to conserve in her the traditions of my life and the order of my discipline.

FATHER: Don't blame yourselves. I do not blame you. The forces from without, which have come like hurricanes from across the sea, are powerful. Hardly a home has not felt them.

GRANDMOTHER: We are as powerful as they. We understand how to sacrifice to save all we hold precious. As in the past, sacrifices were made—as in the past.

FATHER: My revered mother—

GRANDMOTHER: Does the child love me?

MOTHER: There is no doubt of that. Ever since she was a child and you brought her pears from the orchard, carved her pumpkin at the Harvest Festival, and presented her with her New Year's sash, she has loved you.

GRANDMOTHER: Then, since it is so, there is some respect, too? Somewhere, deep in her heart?

MOTHER: Oh, there is. She is not a wicked child. Only headstrong and easily swayed by something new. This will pass. I pray it will pass and she will be a helpmate to her husband and win respect at the shrines of her ancestors.

GRANDMOTHER: It may pass. But not unless my generation sets an example.

FATHER: Sets an example, my mother?

GRANDMOTHER: That is what we have failed to do. We have been self-indulgent and complacent, thinking our ways safe against time and influence. We have failed to renew the old faith, have failed to sacrifice everything for our beliefs to show how greatly the heart may be swayed by duty. We have lost courage.

FATHER: My mother—

GRANDMOTHER: You know my meaning. It is the ancient, accepted way. It is the only way I know to right a wrong in the eyes of the gods and in the eyes of our watchful forebears. Otherwise, I am helpless and can make no protest except with the cawing tongue of an old woman, which no one heeds.

[*She rises and moves slowly towards exit, right, as*

the MOTHER *and* FATHER *bow low in profound respect.*]

FATHER: We will worship at your shrine, noble Mother.

GRANDMOTHER: I thank you, my son. I will keep my watch over you. [*She bows and exits.*]

FATHER: Bring our daughter here.

[*The* MOTHER *bows and exits, left.*

[*The* FATHER *stands, looking at the shrine intently as if trying to read the secret of life in the calm and gracious features of the timeless Buddha.*

[*Enter* DAUGHTER *and* MOTHER *from left. The* MOTHER *goes to the shrine, kneels before the Buddha and remains immobile during the following.*]

FATHER [*gently*]: My daughter, your hair was beautiful a few short minutes ago.

DAUGHTER [*subdued and exhausted*]: Yes.

FATHER: Do you recall, as a child, how mortified you were when the ends of your hair would curl instead of hanging straight like other little girls'?

DAUGHTER: I remember.

FATHER: Do you remember, as well, who it was who studied in old books, who made up the sticky solution, and who bought a special stiff brush with her rice-cake money? Who sat patiently hour upon hour, combing and brushing and combing again, and brushing a thousand times over, so that your hair would be straight?

DAUGHTER: It was Grandmother.

FATHER: And do you know why she did that?

DAUGHTER: To make my hair straight.

FATHER: More than that. It was to save you from shame. To set you an example of sacrifice and duty. She knew that if your hair was not straight your family would be ridiculed as well as you. And it is a woman's duty to save the honour of her family however she can. In small matters—and in great.

DAUGHTER: I can't help it if I don't think the way everyone else does.

FATHER: Honour is the same for us all.

DAUGHTER: Honour—?

FATHER: It is a word you have heard many times. Have you understood what it meant?

DAUGHTER [*petulantly*]: Oh, I don't know.

FATHER: Honour is the high reputation which we deserve, not by always being right, but by always living with respect and in accord with true principles.

DAUGHTER: How do you know when a principle is true?

FATHER: Perhaps you must look into the deeps of your heart to see how full its meaning is.

[*There is a noise off, right, as of an instrument falling to the floor.*

[*The* MOTHER *rises unobtrusively from the shrine and exits, centre back.*]

DAUGHTER: I believe all I have said.

FATHER: Do you believe in it strongly?

DAUGHTER: Yes, I do.

FATHER: With courage?

DAUGHTER: Yes.

FATHER: Enough to sacrifice for it?

DAUGHTER: Yes.

FATHER: Enough to sacrifice—supremely?

[*The* MOTHER *appears at right. She bows low.*]

MOTHER: My honoured husband, your revered mother is now with her ancestors. [*She kneels in prayer, facing the inner room, right.*]

DAUGHTER [*staggered*]: *My grandmother—? My grandmother—?*

FATHER: Yes.

DAUGHTER: Gone—to the other world?

FATHER: It was by her own choice and by her own hand.

DAUGHTER: Father—why? Oh, Father, why?

FATHER: Because she believed and had no other protest against your disbelief.

DAUGHTER [*going slowly, as if hypnotized, towards exit, right*]: Against—my—disbelief—?

FATHER: Yes, go in to her, so that sacrifice and honour will no longer be only words to you.

[*The* DAUGHTER *exits right. The* FATHER *goes to*

the shrine and kneels before it.

[*After a few moments the* DAUGHTER *enters from right, in the extreme agitation of her horror.*]

DAUGHTER: Mother! Mother! [*The* MOTHER *does not move. The* DAUGHTER *runs across to the* FATHER.] My father! My father! [*He does not move. She turns and comes down-stage.*] I believe—I believe— [*She falls down onto a cushion. In a wail of anguish:*] Oh, I don't know what I believe.

[*She is sobbing and beating her hands, as the curtain falls.*]

Lament for Harmonica (Maya)

GWEN PHARIS RINGWOOD

CHARACTERS

In the Order of Appearance

JOSEPHINA SAMUEL, *an old Shushwap woman*
MARTHA PAUL, *her friend*
MRS. ROLAND, *an agency worker*
MAYA SAMUEL *(pronounced May-ya)*
ELLEN, *Martha's niece*
GILBERT, *an Indian*
ALLAN, *a white man*

Time: The present. Late evening in spring.

Place: The doorstep and clearing outside JOSEPHINA'S *cabin on the reserve.*

Scene: The reservation is set in a valley surrounded by high rhythmic hills. Back centre is indicated the shape of a high-steepled church against the darkening sky.

A section of weathered log fence (corral type) cuts across the upstage left corner. Down left another section of fence runs somewhat parallel to the upstage piece. Between may be a broken gate.

Down right is the doorway and stoop or porch of a worn log house. The porch slopes slightly. Two 2 x 4

*pillars support a light roof. The porch has been swept
and is not cluttered.*

*Center stage (downstage centre) is a low camp fire
with a black pot suspended on a stick above the rock en-
closure for the fire. On either side of the fire are rough
wooden benches. The legs for the bench consist of two
round sections of logs.*

*This setting may be simplified by using only the
benches, fire, and indicating the porch and doorway.*

As the play opens MARTHA *and* JOSEPHINA *are sitting
one on either side of the fire,* JOSEPHINA *on the bench at
stage right. From a house off stage comes the sad thin
sound of a harmonica very well played . . . the unseen
player improvises a plaintive tune, slides into some cowboy folk song, then returns to his improvisation. Somewhere in another long house the player, a boy of fifteen,
lies on a ragged mattress, looking up at the chinks of
light that filter through the roof, and plays his music.
The sound recurs from time to time during the play and
is never obtrusive, merely a part of the place.*

MARTHA *wears a dark cotton print dress, almost to
her ankles, and heavy shoes. She has a dark shawl or
jacket around her shoulders. Her hair is tied back. She
is smoking a cigarette.* MARTHA *is about 60 years old.*

JOSEPHINA *is dressed in a long dark skirt, dark blouse
and shapeless sweater. Heavy low black shoes and dark
stockings. Her hair is in two long braids and is very
black. She is older than* MARTHA. *She is broad and
stocky with a strong patient face.*

*When the two women speak they speak usually with-
out much inflection, and with a slower rhythm than
white people use.*

JOSEPHINA *moves to the fire and, lifting a lid off the
pot, stirs at the soup she is making.*

JOSEPHINA: On such a warm night, we don't need the
fire.

MARTHA: It keeps off the mosquitoes, Josephina,
and when the sun's gone, the fire feels good.

JOSEPHINA: And it keeps the soup hot. You want some soup, Martha?

MARTHA [*nodding*]: I want some. [*After a brief pause.*] Maya went past my house.

JOSEPHINA [*ladling soup into an enamel cup*]: She did?

MARTHA: She never stops now. She goes right by.

JOSEPHINA: She's always in a hurry.

MARTHA: I suppose she was hitchhiking into town.

JOSEPHINA [*giving* MARTHA *the soup and getting some for herself*]: That's right.

MARTHA: She goes to town every day now. Does she have a job?

JOSEPHINA: She did have, but she quit.

MARTHA: You should make her work.

JOSEPHINA: She don't listen to me. Since her child died, Maya spends all her time in town. It was bad for her when he died, Martha. Now she don't care what she does.

MARTHA: It was bad for you too, Josephina, losing a great-grandson. Now you have only Maya.

JOSEPHINA [*sitting down with her soup*]: The house is empty without the child.

MARTHA: In the old days I remember many got sick as he did. At sun rise they would be well and walking about and when the sun set they would be gone.

JOSEPHINA: You know, Martha, on the morning Maya's boy died, a whiskey-jack flew round the fire here three times, crying as he flew. Always my grandmother said that was a sign of death.

MARTHA [*solemnly*]: The old ones were not fools.

JOSEPHINA: And the night before he died, a black lizard crossed my path and went under the old church. That too is a bad sign.

MARTHA: The priest would not like to hear that. He would tell you to go down on your knees and pray.

JOSEPHINA: I pray. And on my knees. But I have not seen Maya on her knees once since the child died.

MARTHA: She is too proud, Josephina. All the young

ones think so. And my niece, Ellen, says Maya drinks
too much too.

JOSEPHINA: I tell her she should not run around or
drink so much but she won't listen. Not to anyone. When
the priest comes she leaves the house.

MARTHA [*putting her cup down and lighting a cigarette*]: Ahh ya, the young are like magpies. They go
screaming from one thing to another. If they find a coloured string, they clatter with joy, as if it were the world.

JOSEPHINA [*with a rueful smile*]: Still it's better to
be young than old, Martha. What's left when you're old
but to remember the old days or sit together railing
against the young, with envy stale in the mouth?
[*Getting up to take* MARTHA'*s cup and her own back to
the ledge on the porch.*] Look at us! Two old women
tossing the hulls of wisdom back and forth. No one else
listens to us.

MARTHA: In the old days people stayed home and
there were stories told around the fire. It was a proud
thing to be old and tell the stories. But not any more.
Yet old as I am I can be glad of warm nights or a fresh
salmon or good soup hot from the fire. [*Smiling at her
friend and pointing knowingly with her finger.*] For us
death is the enemy, Josephina, not age. And death takes
even the young some times.

JOSEPHINA: Yes, you are right, Martha. [JOSEPHINA
stands, remembering.] I thought she'd cry out, pray, or
weep for her boy but she stood there, silent as a stone.
"Maya," I said, "Maya, come away." Still she stood silent with a gray face. [*She looks at* MARTHA *then.*] I
never saw her weep.

MARTHA: Did the man—his father—ever come or
send her money?

JOSEPHINA [*turning away impatiently and rinsing out
cups at water barrel on the stoop*]: How do I know?

MARTHA: She won't say who he is?

JOSEPHINA: No. He's white, like her father was.
That's all I know.

[*She brings from the back of the barrel a basket*

*containing some pieces of buckskin, a sharp knife
and coloured silks down to her bench.*]

MARTHA: Does Maya give you money?

JOSEPHINA: Some.

MARTHA: · She has good clothes.

JOSEPHINA: Yes.

[*She takes out a piece of leather cut in the shape of
a glove and begins working on it.*]

MARTHA [*unwilling to drop the subject*]: My niece
says Maya is bad. She says Maya is a—

JOSEPHINA [*angrily*]: Your niece hates Maya. Ellen
wants Gilbert for herself and Gilbert only looks at
Maya. You know that. Ellen has been jealous of Maya
since they were children.

MARTHA: Ellen is jealous all right. She's afraid Maya
will marry Gilbert.

JOSEPHINA: I wish she would. Gilbert is a good boy.
He can work hard.

MARTHA: He's a good rider.

JOSEPHINA: He can get a job on a ranch any time.

MARTHA: She would be lucky to marry Gilbert.

JOSEPHINA: I don't know about Maya, Martha.
[*With controlled feeling.*] I don't know what will happen.

MARTHA: She is too clever, I guess.

JOSEPHINA: She was the brightest student from the
reserve, the only one to finish High School.

MARTHA [*without emotion*]: Running with the whites
always brings us trouble.

JOSEPHINA: For all her white blood, Maya wanted to
be Indian. She would come home from school and ask
me how they did things in the old days, how my grandmother cooked or made the clothes, what stories the old
ones told. She wrote down the stories in a book she had.
At night she begged me to sing the war songs or the pot-
latch songs, but I couldn't remember them. Or she
would say, "Show me the dog dance or the chicken
dance. Show me how they made the wolf mask." When I
couldn't show her she looked at me as if I'd robbed her
somehow.

MARTHA [*comforting her*]: None of us remember.

JOSEPHINA [*indicating the glove*]: I am making her gloves. I can do that. I know the old designs.

MARTHA: They take too long to make.

JOSEPHINA: When she was a child I thought Maya would bring great honour to me. Now she don't care what she does. She hides behind her eyes even from me who raised her. She won't listen to me.

[MRS. ROLAND, *an efficient, pleasant woman, comes in from off stage right through the gate. She looks uncertainly at* JOSEPHINA *and* MARTHA.]

MRS. ROLAND: Hello. Is one of you Mrs. Samuel? Josephina Samuel?

JOSEPHINA [*remaining seated*]: That's my name.

MRS. ROLAND [*approaching them*]: I'm Mrs. Roland from the Agency. And this is— [*She smiles.*]

JOSEPHINA: Mrs. Paul.

MRS. ROLAND: How do you do, Mrs. Paul. [*She shakes hands with* MARTHA.] Mrs. Samuel, is your granddaughter at home?

JOSEPHINA [*warily*]: No. She's not here.

MRS. ROLAND: Where could I find her?

JOSEPHINA: I don't know.

MARTHA: She's in town.

MRS. ROLAND: I see. Will she be home soon?

JOSEPHINA: I don't know when she's coming back.

MRS. ROLAND: She'll be here tomorrow?

JOSEPHINA: I think she will.

MRS. ROLAND: I'll have to come back tomorrow then. [*She turns to go, then changes her mind.*] May I sit down, Mrs. Samuel?

JOSEPHINA: Sure.

MRS. ROLAND: I'll tell you why I want to see Maya. We want her to go back to school, to University this fall.

JOSEPHINA [*unenthusiastic*]: I don't think she would go to school any more. She finished school.

MRS. ROLAND: We want her to train for a teacher.

JOSEPHINA: Maya's too old to go to school. She's nineteen.

MRS. ROLAND: Nineteen isn't old, Mrs. Samuel.

JOSEPHINA: Besides, it costs money.

MRS. ROLAND: The Agency has the money. We've got a special grant for outstanding students. Your granddaughter is the first on the list from this reservation.

JOSEPHINA: She should get married.

MRS. ROLAND: That could come later. She could come back here and teach. We need Indian teachers.

JOSEPHINA [obstinately]: I need her home to help me.

MRS. ROLAND: You wouldn't stand in the way of her chance to get a good job, Mrs. Samuel?

JOSEPHINA: Maya is all I have. My son died in the war. My daughter, her mother, died at Coquilitza.

MRS. ROLAND: Mrs. Samuel, she's a brilliant student. You must give her this chance.

JOSEPHINA: I don't think she would want to go.

MRS. ROLAND [annoyed]: I'll talk to her tomorrow. Please realize that this is good for Maya.

JOSEPHINA: I'll tell her you came to see her.

MRS. ROLAND: And why I came.

JOSEPHINA: I'll tell her.

MRS. ROLAND: Give her these papers please. They explain the terms of the grant. We can fill out her application tomorrow. [She gives a large envelope to JOSEPHINA.] Goodbye, Mrs. Paul. Goodbye, Mrs. Samuel.

MARTHA: Goodbye.

MRS. ROLAND [at gate]: Don't hold your granddaughter here. She needs this chance.

JOSEPHINA: I don't know what she'll do.

[MRS. ROLAND goes out, disconcerted and annoyed. There is a pause. JOSEPHINA looks at the papers, puts them in the basket.]

JOSEPHINA: Maya will read these, I guess.

MARTHA: She should stay home with you now and take care of you.

JOSEPHINA: I think she won't go.

MARTHA: You're getting old.

JOSEPHINA: I can still work.

MARTHA: The white people I worked for at Soda

Creek sent their girl to that school. It costs much money.

JOSEPHINA: You heard her say the Agency would pay.

MARTHA: If the whites know how Maya is always drinking and running around with tramps, I don't think they'd pay money for her to go.

JOSEPHINA [*resentfully*]: They know she is bright.

MARTHA: She should be married now.

JOSEPHINA [*turning away*]: She needs something. I don't know . . .

MARTHA: You could take Maya away. She should stay with you.

JOSEPHINA: Take her where?

MARTHA: To your sister's place at Alkali. If the white woman finds you gone, she won't bother. They forget soon. In the fall you could come back here.

JOSEPHINA: She said she was coming back tomorrow.

MARTHA: Go early in the morning. Gilbert can take you.

JOSEPHINA: I think you are right, Martha. Maya should stay with me.

MARTHA: Will you show her that paper?

JOSEPHINA: No. I'll throw it in the fire. [*She throws the envelope in the fire.*] There. It will soon burn up.

[*There is a sound of a car approaching off stage. It stops and young voices shout and laugh.*]

MARTHA: Listen!

MAYA [*off stage*]: Wait for me. Don't go without me, you promise?

VOICE [*off stage*]: We'll give you five minutes.

SECOND VOICE: Taxis cost money, Maya.

MAYA: Gilbert's got money, haven't you, Gilbert? Pay him.

[*There is more laughter, slightly ribald and drunken.*]

MAYA: Come on, Gilbert, you can help me!

MALE VOICE [*off*]: Let me help you, Maya. I'll help!

MARTHA [*getting up*]: I'll be going.

JOSEPHINA [*urgently*]: No, you stay, Martha.

[MAYA *appears in the gateway. She is a beautiful girl, quite tall, dark with a golden skin, rich full mouth, dark eyes. She is wearing a bright sheath that has been torn from the sleeve across the back. She is vivid, hard and angry under her cynical gaiety. She has been drinking. Her hair is somewhat disheveled. She is carrying a light coat and under it has concealed a small bottle of whiskey.*]

MAYA: Here I am, Grandmother! A poor thing but thine own!

JOSEPHINA: You're drunk, Maya.

MAYA [*laughing, pretending to be shocked*]: Oh no! No! Am I drunk, Gilbert?

[GILBERT *has come in behind* MAYA. *He is very dark, all Indian, quiet. He wears blue jeans, light cowboy shirt, good boots.*]

MAYA: We brought you a present. See! [*She holds up the bottle.*] To give you nice dreams!

JOSEPHINA: Get in the house.

MAYA: No.

JOSEPHINA: Why did you let her drink so much, Gilbert?

MAYA [*leaning lightly on* GILBERT's *shoulder*]: Leave Gilbert alone. He wants to marry me. Shall I marry Gilbert, Grandmother, and live like a queen in Gilbert's castle?

JOSEPHINA [*moving to* MAYA]: Look at you! Your dress is torn.

MAYA: I came home to change.

JOSEPHINA: You're not to go back in town!

MAYA: I will go back. The taxi's waiting for me. Don't you want your present?

JOSEPHINA [*taking the bottle*]: Where did you get the money to buy this?

MAYA: Gilbert has money. He took all the money in the bronc riding Sunday. He rode like a wildcat, didn't you, Gilbert? He has lots of money. [*She smiles at him provocatively, then her expression changes quickly to mockery.*] But not enough to buy Maya, have you, Gilbert? Oh, I'm for sale, but the price is too high yet. That's so, Martha. Some pay for virginity. Some want experience! Gilbert just wants Maya!

JOSEPHINA [*pushing* MAYA *on the shoulder*]: Go in and change, Maya. Now!

MAYA [*angrily shrugging her off*]: Keep your hands off of me. I won't be pushed. I'll do what I like. [*To* GILBERT.] Wait for me.

   [MAYA *goes into the cabin.*]

JOSEPHINA: What happened?

GILBERT [*awkwardly*]: Maya was in the beer parlor with some others. I wasn't there then. She started to sing some Indian song. They told her to be quiet and she swore at them. The beer slinger grabbed her and was going to push her out and he tore her dress. She bit his hand and he was yelling like a pig.

JOSEPHINA: Did he get the police on Maya?

GILBERT: No. I brought her home then to change her dress.

JOSEPHINA: You don't let her drink any more, Gilbert. She should stay home now.

GILBERT: It's early. We were going to the drive-in.

JOSEPHINA: Do you have to work tomorrow?

GILBERT: I told Johnson I'd fix fences.

JOSEPHINA: I thought you'd borrow your uncle's car and take me and Maya to Alkali in the morning.

GILBERT: I could do that.

JOSEPHINA: The Agency wants to send Maya away. I'll take her to my sister.

GILBERT: What time?

JOSEPHINA: About six o'clock.

GILBERT: I'll tell Johnson I'm not coming.

   [ELLEN, *a thin, rather untidy Indian girl, comes in from left.*]

ELLEN: Come on, Gilbert. The taxi man wants to get back to town. Let's go. Hello, Aunt Martha.

MARTHA: You should stay home too, Ellen.

ELLEN: The night's young. Come on, Gilbert.

GILBERT: Maya won't be long.

ELLEN: You'd wait for her if she took all night.

GILBERT: It's not your business what I do.

ELLEN: Do you think she cares two cents for you except when you have money to spend?

MARTHA: Ellen—you had best leave it alone.

ELLEN: I won't. To Maya he's the dirt under her feet. How can you be such a fool?

GILBERT: Go on back to the others.

ELLEN: You've seen him, Josephina! How on a Sunday he always looks to see if Maya's watching the chutes. He puts on his white shirt, polishes his forty-dollar boots, walks out smoking a cigarette, leans on the fence and waits for the meanest bronc they've got—all to show off for Maya!

GILBERT: You don't know about me.

ELLEN [fiercely]: I know. I've watched you. I've watched you straddle the bucking horse, your knees tight to the wet flanks, and you twist as the horse twists, thinking that Maya smiles her slow smile to see you. She doesn't even notice you, Gilbert. She doesn't care whether you're thrown or broken or make a good ride to the whistle. She doesn't hold a thought for you. She uses you, that's all. Why do you risk your neck for her?

GILBERT: Go on. Leave me alone.

ELLEN: Yes. Leave you to dream of Maya. Well, dream small, that's all she's worth. [She has taken hold of his sleeve.]

GILBERT [pushing her off]: Shut up, Ellen.

ELLEN: Maya's a slut, you know it. She bore one white man's bastard. Perhaps she'll get another for you to feed. She'll spend your money but she sleeps with white men!

GILBERT [slaps her]: Get out!

[MAYA appears on the step of the cabin.]

MAYA: No, let her stay. What Ellen says is true. I am a slut. [Her tone is disinterested and low.] I—I thought to be something different—not that it matters. [She picks up the enamel cup, goes to the bottle on the bench and pours a drink.] Here's to you, Ellen. [She drinks.] If Gilbert wants you he has only to say so. I've no hold on him. Take her, Gilbert. What she is, you know. You can count on it. She's a wasp—but faithful. What I am, I don't know myself. Do you know, Gilbert?

GILBERT: I don't care.

MAYA: I care. Sometimes at school I'd read things. I learned fast, didn't I, Grandmother? I liked to learn. Sometimes I thought I'd find a book, some book somewhere to tell me some answers, show me what to look for, but there is no book. [*She looks at* GILBERT.] What love I had, I gave. I'm no good for you. Go on, I'm not coming.

> [GILBERT *looks at her uncertainly. There is a silence. The sound of the harmonica is faint and plaintive in the distance. In sudden anger* MAYA *advances on* ELLEN *and* GILBERT.]

MAYA: Get out! Get out! I don't want you here. I'm alone, I tell you. I'll always be alone. [*To* MARTHA.] You too . . . Go! I don't believe your books, your prayers, your songs. I don't believe them, hear me? [*To the old woman.*] I hate your old faces, I hate your lips like dried leaves and your trembling hands and your eyes rimmed red with cataracts. I hate it all. We're ants crawling under the sky and the journey we take means nothing. Get out, I tell you.

> [GILBERT *and* ELLEN *go out left.* MARTHA *goes slowly out right.*]

MAYA [*to* JOSEPHINA]: And you believe the prayers they taught you. You and your Latin and your rosary. When your son died you said the mass and when my mother died. And when my son died you prayed and wept. For eighty years you've lived on a crust of bread and some white men's prayers. And that's a life, a destiny! Well, it's not enough. I hate it, I tell you, I hate it! [*More quietly and with great self-loathing.*] Look at me. Shall I bleed now or wait till after? Take my harmonica and dream at night of songs I almost heard, sing of how deep the frost lies on the golden heart while Time, the ape, sits grinning at the wheel. Do you know what that means—nothing, like your Latin, Grandma! Me, I'm an Indian. I'll show them. I'm an Indian, stretched on a plain as barren as a burnt-out star. To hell with them all, I'll show them! [*After a pause, in a broken tone.*] I wanted something. I wanted to be different. Here I am!

JOSEPHINA: Maya, tomorrow we'll go away, to Alkali or up the valley. We'll go into the woods and mountains, fish for salmon, hunt berries and trail the young deer, like in the old days. That will heal you.

MAYA: Oh Grandmother, I'm no good, for you or anyone.

JOSEPHINA: Gilbert will take us.

MAYA: It's no use.

JOSEPHINA: You'll come with me, Maya.

MAYA: No. I don't belong there. I'd get restless. I'd say things and they'd hate me and take it out on you. I won't go, Grandmother. You go.

[*A pause. The harmonica is heard again. After a while,* JOSEPHINA *reluctantly makes up her mind to speak.*]

JOSEPHINA: Would you want to go away to school?

MAYA: Now? You talk foolish.

JOSEPHINA: A woman from the Agency was here. She said they had the money to send you.

MAYA: Where? They've got nothing on me.

JOSEPHINA: To University, she said. To be a teacher.

MAYA: Me? A teacher. Now! Don't make me laugh. [*Pause.*] I would like to teach.

JOSEPHINA: She said you were the first from this reserve. She thinks you don't belong here with these people.

MAYA: They're my people, whether I belong or not.

JOSEPHINA: She's coming tomorrow to see you. I threw the papers she brought in the fire. You're all I have now, Maya, and I'm old.

MAYA: I would come back here.

JOSEPHINA: It's hard to be old and alone, Maya. I haven't anyone but you.

MAYA: I know. I won't leave. I'm going in.

[*Abruptly* MAYA *goes into the house, closing the door after her.* JOSEPHINA, *looking old and wor-*

*ried, banks the fire, then turns to move towards the
porch. As she nears it her eye catches something
upstage of the stoop. She raises her stick, and
speaks in a low tone with awe and terror.*]

JOSEPHINA: Get out, you black lizard! Get away!
I'll kill you! [*But her hand remains raised, clenching
the stick, as she looks down.*] Go . . . Go away from
us. Leave us alone.

[ALLAN, *a white man, enters from the road. He is
in his middle twenties, good-looking with a sensi-
tive, rather weak face.*]

ALLAN: I beg pardon, I'm looking for someone, a girl
named Maya Samuel.

JOSEPHINA: What do you want with her? [*She turns,
startled.*]

ALLAN [*resenting her tone*]: I want to see her. Do
you know her?

JOSEPHINA: She's my granddaughter.

ALLAN [*taken aback*]: Oh. Oh, I see. Maya lives
here?

JOSEPHINA: What do you want with her?

ALLAN [*trying to win her confidence*]: I knew her
one summer. I was making a trip through here and
thought I'd look her up.

JOSEPHINA: She's not here.

ALLAN: Where could I find her?

JOSEPHINA: I don't know.

ALLAN: I want to see her.

JOSEPHINA: She's gone.

ALLAN: Where? Where is she? [JOSEPHINA *is silent.*]
Look, is it a crime to look up a friend?

JOSEPHINA [*slowly*]: It was you she went with three
years ago, when I was sick. [*Pause.*] It was you, wasn't
it? [*Another pause.*] She was sixteen.

ALLAN: I didn't know that then. She said she was
older.

JOSEPHINA: She just finished high school. After you
left she went to learn typing and business.

ALLAN: I know.

JOSEPHINA: She was back home before Christmas. She had a child.

ALLAN: She never told me that.

JOSEPHINA: She wrote to you.

ALLAN: She didn't tell me about the child. Why didn't you write? You could have had someone write?

JOSEPHINA: She wouldn't say your name.

ALLAN: I'm sorry. I should have answered her letter but I got busy and—

JOSEPHINA: You are no good for Maya.

ALLAN: Look, I've got to see her. Tell me where she is.

JOSEPHINA: No. She's had enough of you. Leave her alone.

[MAYA *comes out, stands looking at* ALLAN. *She is smoking. There is a long silence except for the music off stage.* MAYA *flips her cigarette away, motions to* JOSEPHINA.]

MAYA: Go in, Grandmother. We'll talk here.

JOSEPHINA: Maya—

MAYA: Please.

[JOSEPHINA *moves past her into the house.* MAYA *waits quietly on the step as she goes in and closes the door.*]

ALLAN: Maya!

MAYA: Hello, Allan. How did you get here?

ALLAN: I've been up north. This is the first time I've been this way since—

MAYA: For three years.

ALLAN: I couldn't come back the next summer. There was no job. I stayed on and worked at the station.

MAYA: Yes.

ALLAN: I wanted to come back. Maya, your grandmother said you had a child, my child. Why didn't you write to me?

MAYA: I wrote.

ALLAN: Just once. I didn't answer, but if you'd told me—

MAYA: She lied. There was no child.

ALLAN: I don't think she lied. Why would she?

MAYA: Why? To get money from you, why else? She's old and greedy and has nothing.

ALLAN: She said—

MAYA: Suppose it were true. Suppose I'd written to say I'm in trouble. Would that have brought you back? Or would you send money and the address for an abortion? Everything fixed up with relief, regards and no regrets. Isn't that the usual way, the white way?

ALLAN: I'd have come, Maya.

MAYA: And if you had, would you believe him yours, seeing my people's eyes look back at you? Oh no. You'd have denied him. We're lucky there was no child.

ALLAN: You swear that?

MAYA: I swear nothing. He'd have been more white than Indian, Allan. Would I have kept him here on the reserve? Or would I give him to some kind barren pair to raise as their own? Soon he'd grow tall in a suburban house, watch the wide screen, and behind his thoughts begin to wonder who he is and why. If I had borne your child, would I have kept him?

ALLAN: For God's sake, Maya, tell me.

MAYA: There was no child. [*Cruelly.*] If there had been I'd have killed him, dashed him from the rock yonder to the river and rid us forever of a summer passion. If there had been a son, I'd have left him to die on a cliff somewhere. Why keep a souvenir of something that doesn't matter?

ALLAN [*shaking her*]: Stop it, Maya, stop!

MAYA [*breaking away from him*]: I have no child. Let your mind rest.

[*A pause as they look at each other.*]

ALLAN: I thought of you all the time after I left. I wanted to come back, meant to come back, and then—

MAYA: Then you got married.

ALLAN: You knew about that?

MAYA: I read it in the papers. I can read, you know. My grandmother doesn't read but I read well. That's progress.

ALLAN: I've never forgot those days in the mountains. Have you?

MAYA: No. Each morning was a promise. Each night when I put my arms around you I felt we were one flesh, one hope. I remember.

ALLAN: I had to come back. I had to see you, even for a few hours, a day.

MAYA: Maybe I put a curse on you, an Indian curse. [*She turns away from him.*]

ALLAN: I've got two days, Maya. I drove night and day to give me time here. I've got two days and money. We can spend them.

MAYA: Sure. We can spend them both.

ALLAN: Get what you need. Let's go.

MAYA: I waited for you the next summer. I'd look at the hills and whisper "how beautiful upon the mountain are the feet of my beloved." And each evening when the trees turned black over the water I'd bargain with tomorrow to bring you back.

ALLAN: I'm here now.

MAYA: Yes.

ALLAN: Let's get out of here.

MAYA: No. It's too late, Allan.

ALLAN: Not for us. Remember.

MAYA: Don't touch me.

ALLAN: What's the matter? I'm here—after three years, Maya. We're together.

MAYA: Three years is a lifetime. You were the first. Do you think you were the last? Look at me. I'm an empty room, despoiled by any passing stranger, gutted of hope and faith and desolate of love—the refuge of the lost, the lonely and the hungry, that's Maya.

ALLAN: Maya, listen. I've come because there's no rest for me without you. You got inside of me. You belong to me.

MAYA: I can belong to any man at all. You don't believe that, do you? Hah, it's easy. Put your arms around them, enfold them, be wife, mother, child, brief respite from the world's woe and let them go. Look at me. Maya, the hill-side whore. Mistress of the toothless and the angry, concubine to the half-wit and the sot, wife to the fumbling and the fearful. I can take them all and leave them and I do! Oh, I'm a foxy doxy, Chicken Little, and the world may end tomorrow, so bestride me, little man, be my Colossus and I'll be your world. That's how it is—it's easy, believe me. Get out now. You've seen me.

ALLAN: No matter what you are, I can't go.

MAYA: Sure. When you stop caring, everything comes.

ALLAN: You haven't stopped caring. You're still waiting for me. You know it. [*He moves towards her, pulls her to him.*]

MAYA [*breaking away*]: Let go. [*She whirls and picks up the knife from* JOSEPHINA's *basket.*] Keep off me. You think because I'm any man's, I'm yours? Not any more, believe that.

ALLAN: I don't believe it. Play hard to get if you want to, Baby . . . I don't mind. [GILBERT *enters from left, stands quietly watching for a moment.* ALLAN *takes* MAYA's *wrist.*] Drop the knife. You couldn't use it if you wanted to. [*The knife falls to the ground.*] That's better.

GILBERT: Leave her alone.

MAYA: Go on, Gilbert. I can look after myself.

ALLAN: Who's he, your husband?

MAYA: He could be.

ALLAN: You could do better.

GILBERT [*moving towards them*]: Get out.

ALLAN: He's drunk.

GILBERT: Sure I'm drunk—

ALLAN: Lay off. [ALLAN *pushes at* GILBERT, *who sways.*]

GILBERT: I'm drunk—and I'm going to kill you.

MAYA: Gilbert, listen to me.

GILBERT: Sure, I'll listen. It's like Ellen says . . . be nice to the whites, they're kind to us. They let us pick up their cigarette butts, wear their cast-off clothes. You've worn them, Maya. We come to their back doors. My mother begged bones from the meat they cooked to feed us. Our women have your children and we feed and clothe your bastards. And Maya put your son to her breast—not mine—and watched him die and waited for you to come but you didn't make a sign.

ALLAN [*to* MAYA]: It's true then.

MAYA: It's true. He died last winter.

GILBERT: Sure, he died. And she becomes a tramp and that's your doing.

MAYA: No, Gilbert. Mine.

GILBERT: So now you've come back to claim your Indian scum—that's what you call us, scum! You'll never get her.

MAYA: Gilbert, go home. Get out of here.

GILBERT: Oh no. Not now. I've waited for this. I think since I was born I've waited. And now my time comes. I'll show you we're not scum. Come on, I'll show you who's a man.

ALLAN: You drunken fool, get out of here. Come back when you're sober. [*He slaps* GILBERT.]

GILBERT: I'm here. I don't have to come back.

[*He suddenly throws* ALLAN *off balance and pushes him to the ground.*]

ALLAN: Take it easy.

GILBERT: They'll take scum to be soldiers, white man. How about that?

MAYA: Let him up now, Gilbert. You've proved enough. Let him up now.

GILBERT: I hate him. I've hated him all my life. I've felt him between my hands.

MAYA: Gilbert, stop . . . For God's sake, stop.

GILBERT: They fondle us like dogs or kick us, take everything. I hate the bastards . . . [*He is almost sobbing.*]

ALLAN: Help . . . he's . . . he's . . .

[GILBERT *is choking him.*]

MAYA [*trying vainly to pull* GILBERT *away*]: No, Gilbert, no . . . no . . . Look, I've got a knife, Gilbert . . . I'll . . .

GILBERT: I'll kill him if I hang for it . . . I've got to kill him . . .

MAYA: Stop. Gilbert. No!

[*Unable to pull* GILBERT *away, she raises the knife*

and stabs down hard. GILBERT *turns, looking at her, letting* ALLAN *go.*]

GILBERT: Maya . . .

MAYA: I had to do it. You were choking him. [ALLAN *gets up.* MAYA *looks at him, her eyes wide with shock.*] Get out, Allan. Please. Get out of here.

ALLAN: You'd better come with me. There'll be trouble.

MAYA: No. Go on . . . Go!

[*She kneels beside* GILBERT. ALLAN *goes out quickly.* JOSEPHINA *comes out of the house, sees* MAYA *kneeling beside* GILBERT.]

GILBERT: I had to get rid of him. He was no good for you. I showed him we aren't scum, didn't I?

MAYA: Yes, you showed him. I saw you.

GILBERT: Then why did you hurt me, Maya?

[*He slumps forward, his head on her knee.* JOSE-PHINA *kneels on the porch, saying a prayer over and over. In the silence the sound of the harmonica drifts across the night.*]

MAYA [*at last*]: He's dead, Grandmother. He won't ride any more, he won't jump on the black bronc, tighten his knees against the twisting flanks or take first money in the chutes on Sunday. He's dead, and I killed him. I killed you, Gilbert. I, Maya— I wanted something. I don't know. I thought to be something different.

[MAYA, *staring dully in front of her, remains kneeling beside* GILBERT *as the plaintive song off stage slips away and the curtains close.*]

The Home for Heroes

a parable in one act by
GEORGE BOWERING

The scene is a large, almost bare room. High on one wall is a bell-shaped LOUDSPEAKER. *There is a high wooden stool (the folksinger type) in the middle of the room. On the wall opposite to the loudspeaker—let us say the loudspeaker is at CL and the punching bag is at CR—is a speed punching bag. No drapes or hangings of any kind, except a blackboard about four feet wide on the wall upstage centre. There is one door UR. It is closed as the play begins. There are no windows.*

MR. ALIGARI, *a short man dressed in a business suit and horn-rim glasses, is sitting on the floor, or rather he looks as if he is half-sitting, half-fallen. His hat, one of those green affairs, that looks as if it has been influenced by an advertisement for Alpine holiday fun, lies on the floor beside him.* ALIGARI *appears to have fallen there, though from no great height. He seems to be just regaining enough consciousness to be able to look around and see where he is. He is in no way injured.*

He gets shakily to his feet. He looks around him, apparently puzzled to find himself in such a strange place. He picks up his hat. He walks around the room, finally coming upon the door. He tries the door, finds it locked. As he turns his back on it, it opens silently, stays part way open for just a moment, then just as silently closes. ALIGARI *walks around the room again, prepares to take*

*a swing at the punching bag, stops himself. He walks
around to the blackboard, picks up a piece of thick
chalk (TV weatherman's type) from the blackboard sill,
prepares to write, stops himself. He walks to the door,
tries it again, finds it locked. He goes to the blackboard
again, prepares to write again, stops himself again. Then
he letters in block: WHERE AM I?*

*He walks around the room again, this time feeling for
secret doors or panels. Then he comes back to the
blackboard, hesitates, picks up a blackboard eraser from
the sill, wipes out the former words, and letters in
block: WHEN AM I?*

LOUDSPEAKER: The time is exactly four-thirty.

ALIGARI: I have to get up at six-thirty. [*Pause.*] I'll
be no good at work in the morning.

LOUD: The time is exactly nine p.m.

ALI [*to* LOUDSPEAKER]: See if you can do any better
with my other question.

[*Silence for fifteen seconds. Then the door opens.
A man enters. He is athletic, dressed in a comic-
strip hero's uniform, in the manner of Superman,
Captain Marvel, etc., complete with a long cape.
The new entrant closes the door behind him, walks
over to the blackboard and erases the lettering with
immaculate care. He then goes to the stool and sits
atop it, looking finally at* ALIGARI.]

THE MAN OF STEEL: You in sports?

ALI [*moving toward the door*]: Weekend golf. A little water skiing.

STEEL: Comics?

ALI [*at the door now*]: What?

STEEL: You in a comic strip?

ALI: Not up till now, no.

[ALIGARI *tries the door. It is still locked. No reaction on the part of* THE MAN OF STEEL.]

STEEL: War?

ALI: No.

STEEL: Books? Movies? Exploring?

ALI [*with some impatience*]: No.

STEEL: Well, what are you in?

ALI: That's precisely what I'd like to know.

STEEL: Aren't you a hero?

ALI: I'm afraid I'm just an ordinary junior executive of a confectionery organization. I'm also a commuter. I'm a husband and a father. During the war I was a conscientious objector. Once I was a waiter on the railway. I have varicose veins, anyway. Not a hero. Not hero material. Not the stuff heroes are made of. Right now I'm probably either late at home or late at the shop. The office. I can't seem to find out where I'm supposed to be because I don't know if it's morning or night.

STEEL: I've got varicose veins. In my legs. In my neck. I've got a boil, too. And I get short of breath from flying.

ALI: I'm disillusioned. Or I would be if I could concentrate on it.

STEEL: You're not a hero, eh?

ALI: I'm a flop. I can't even sell candies, or so my wife says. [*He adds as a confidential explanation.*] I'm a daydreamer, she says.

STEEL: Well, what are you doing here?

ALI: I don't have the slightest idea. Why don't you ask him? [*He gestures toward the* LOUDSPEAKER.]

LOUD: The time is exactly twelve-fifteen.

> [*As if that were a signal,* THE MAN OF STEEL *gets off the stool, goes to the blackboard, and letters in large blocks:* THE MAN OF STEEL. ALIGARI *sits on the stool, puts his hat on his head, watching distractedly.*]

LOUD: Look! Up! Up in the sky! It's a bird!

STEEL: I know, now. [*To* ALIGARI.] You're still in your secret identity.

ALI: I'll say.

LOUD: Faster than a speeding bullet!

> [THE MAN OF STEEL *runs in a ludicrous stumbling gait around the room, a look of haggard desperate pride on his face.*]

LOUD: The Man of Steel!

[THE MAN OF STEEL *swings mightily at the punching bag, misses completely, sprawls on the floor.*]

ALI [*to* LOUDSPEAKER]: Leave him alone!

STEEL [*miserably*]: Aren't you going to help me up?

[ALIGARI *goes over and helps* THE MAN OF STEEL *to his feet, then walks away from him in disgust.*]

STEEL [*petulantly*]: Well, how would *you* like it? I'd sell my soul not to be a hero, believe *you* me. The first chance I got, so help me—

[*Stuck for the word or name, he stops. He walks hurriedly over to the blackboard, hurriedly wipes it clean. Then he leaves the room in a hangdog manner.*

[ALIGARI *once more tries the door, once more finds it locked. He lights a cigarette, having trouble with the matches, using three or four matches before the cigarette lights at last. Puzzled, he wets an index finger and holds it up in the air. There is no breeze. He shrugs his shoulders.*]

LOUD: No smoking! Absolutely no smoking, please!

[ALIGARI *drops his cigarette on the floor, steps it out.*]

LOUD: You may smoke if you like.

[ALIGARI *does not smoke. He has his back to the door as a second man enters and sits on the stool. This is a robust man in a baseball uniform, complete except for team insignia. He carries a heavy baseball bat.*]

THE SULTAN OF SWAT [*diffidently*]: Want an autograph?

ALI [*turning to look at him*]: You too? What are you doing here? What did you ever do to be here?

SULTAN: I?

ALI: You. Both of you. All of you, I guess.

SULTAN: Well, why not? Didn't you ever get a stomach ache from eating a lot of something you like a lot? And you can't help it. You never think of the stomach ache till you have it.

ALI: Mmm. Well, I don't deserve a stomach ache or

any kind of ache. I shouldn't be here at all. Somebody has obviously made a mistake.

SULTAN: Oh, really?

ALI: Tough luck, big fellow.

SULTAN: I can't do a thing right since I got traded into this league.

ALI: Ah well, tomorrow is another day.

SULTAN: Don't say that!

[SULTAN *goes into a fit of violent laughter, picking up his bat and swinging it around his head. Still laughing, he swings it at the punching bag and misses. Immediately his laughter stops and he stands still, his back to the audience, the bat drooping from his loose arm.*]

LOUD: The time is Tuesday, October the fourth.

[SULTAN *immediately goes to the blackboard and wipes it clean. He goes to the door with his bat dragging behind him.*]

SULTAN [*as he is going out the door*]: Ever had your picture in the paper?

[*He goes out and closes the door.*]

ALI: In the company magazine once, a group picture of the bowling team.

LOUD: Have your return route ticket stubs ready, please. [ALIGARI *takes a handful of paper money out of his billfold, holds it ready.*] Attention! All flights have been cancelled.

[*A third hero enters the room. He is large, husky, has a fan-shaped white beard, not very long. He wears aviator-type glasses with large panes and steel rims. He is dressed in safari fashion—shorts, puttees, boots, shirt, hunting vest, peaked cap, all in khaki. He is carrying a high-powered rifle with a scope sight over one shoulder, a portable typewriter without a case dangling from the other hand.*[1]

[*He puts his typewriter on the stool, leans his rifle*

---

[1] The description fits the writer Ernest Hemingway as he looked in his later years.

*against a wall. He pulls a large cigar from his vest
pocket and lights it.*]

ALI: How can you be here? I thought you were—
[*Hesitant.*]

PAPA: What did you think I was?

ALI: Well, God, I guess. That is, a lot of people
thought you were. Still do, I guess. I've never really
read—

PAPA: You have no wine.

ALI: No, I haven't got a thing.

PAPA: Too many people haven't.

ALI: I don't even know where I am. Am I in Africa
now?

PAPA: I liked Africa. A man sees a new country and
he likes it. He knows it is good. It is like a woman who
accepts her man and his clean love. I liked the people
and the land, but it is the land you learn to like first.
Then you can begin to like the people. I liked Africa as
soon as I woke up my first morning in camp and had my
first whiskey. The first one is the best. I could fish and
hunt there.

ALI: I always wanted to go to Africa.

PAPA: Every country is good. It is the men who
make a country bad.

ALI: Is it good here?

LOUD: The time is exactly eleven-fourteen.

[PAPA *steps his cigar out, goes to the blackboard,
and letters in large blocks: PAPA.*

[PAPA *picks up his rifle, readies it for firing, stands
as if looking across a plain.*]

LOUD: Bhwana! Look, the big cat! [PAPA *aims the
rifle.*] No, Bhwana, over there! [PAPA *aims the rifle in
the opposite direction.*] No. Bhwana, that is the car!

[PAPA *takes off his glasses, leans the rifle against
his leg, takes out a large khaki handkerchief and
wipes the glasses, puts them on. He looks out over
the plain again, then up at the loudspeaker. Then
he takes the glasses off and puts them in his pocket. He picks up the rifle and aims it at the loudspeaker.*]

LOUD [*laughing*]: Ha ha ha ha ha.

[PAPA *squeezes the trigger. There is a loud click. He squeezes it again and again. After each click there is a short burst of laughter from the* LOUD-SPEAKER. PAPA *drops the rifle to the floor and stands with his head down, carefully avoiding looking at* ALIGARI, *who is behind him.*]

LOUD: Bhwana! Look, the elephant!

[PAPA *goes to the typewriter, sits on the stool with the machine on his lap. He takes a sheet of paper from a pocket, puts it in the machine. He thinks for a while, then, very slowly, with a great show of choosing the right key, taps it once.*]

LOUD: Dark laughter again, Bhwana.

[PAPA *pulls the sheet of paper from the machine, and puts it back in his pocket.*]

ALI [*quietly*]: Too bad about the big cat.

PAPA [*still in character*]: Tomorrow we will shoot again.

ALI: I'm sorry you didn't get him today.

PAPA [*breaking character, peevishly*]: Ah, the shooting's lousy around here. You haven't got a chance. I shoulda stayed in India, for cat's sake.

[PAPA *walks out of the room, dragging the rifle on the floor and carrying the typewriter dangling from one arm.*]

ALI: Buenas tardes.[2]

LOUD [*as the door slams shut*]: Buenas tardes.

[*Resolutely*, ALIGARI *tests the door again, finds it locked. He walks restlessly around the room, glancing expectantly at the door and the* LOUD-SPEAKER. *He stops in front of the punching bag, starts to swing his fist at it, arrests his fist just before he would have hit it. He walks to the stool and sits on it. He notices the lettering on the blackboard, gets up and wipes it off. He returns to the stool and sits on it.*]

---

[2] Spanish for "good afternoon." Hemingway had a great love of things Spanish and set some of his stories in Spain.

LOUD: Take a ten-minute smoke break.

ALI [*sarcastically*]: Many thanks. [*Lights a cigarette.*]

LOUD: No smoking, please.

[ALIGARI *blows smoke toward the* LOUDSPEAK-
ER. *A piercing siren noise from the* LOUDSPEAKER.
ALIGARI *squashes his cigarette on the floor. The si-
ren noise stops.*]

ALI: Well, come on, let's get on with it. [*Nothing
happens.*] Come on, trot out your next object lesson.

LOUD: No spitting.

ALI: Who's spitting?

LOUD: Keep off the grass.

ALI: What grass?

LOUD: No swimming beyond this point.

ALI: What is this point?

LOUD: No passing in this lane. City by-law.

ALI: Aw, shut up.

[*More siren noise from loudspeaker.*]

ALI [*yelling*]: I'm sorry!

LOUD: Post no bills.

ALI [*despondent*]: Do not feed the animals.

LOUD: No trespassing.

ALI: No fishing.

LOUD: No hunting.

ALI: No parking.

LOUD: No stop.

ALI: No sale.

LOUD: No dice.

ALI: No soap.

LOUD: No.

ALI: No.

LOUD: No.

ALI: No.

LOUD: No.

ALI [*after a slight pause, getting to his feet and
shouting*]: *Yes!*

LOUD: No.

ALI [*louder*]: *Y-e-e-e-ssss!*

[*Siren noise.* THE MAN OF STEEL, THE SULTAN OF

SWAT, *and* PAPA *dash into thé room. They stand together, watching* ALIGARI. *The siren noise stops.*]

LOUD: The time is exactly eleven fifty-seven. ·

ALIGARI *goes to the blackboard, picks up chalk, and letters in large blocks*: DANIEL ALIGARI. *He looks at his wristwatch, letters*: THE TIME IS 4:30.

[*The four men look up at the silent loudspeaker. The silence lies heavy in the room. Finally*:

[ALIGARI *coughs*.

[THE MAN OF STEEL *coughs*.

[PAPA *coughs*.

[THE SULTAN OF SWAT *coughs*.]

ALI [*looking at his watch*]: Four thirty-one, now.

SULTAN: Four thirty-one.

PAPA: Four thirty-one is a good time.

STEEL: They said it is eleven fifty-seven.

SULTAN: But he says it is four thirty-one.

[*They all look at* ALIGARI.]

ALI: Standard time.

PAPA: It is good to have a standard time.

LOUD: You are all confined to barracks until further notice.

[*All but* ALIGARI *start to leave*.]

ALI: Wait! [*They stop*.] Why don't you all wait right here? I'm going to wait right here.

[*They look at one another*.]

STEEL: They said we have to be confined to barracks.

ALI: I say: why? Why don't you just stick right here and see what happens?

PAPA: It never happens. *Nothing* ever happens to you.

ALI [*looks around the room, like a strategy-minded general reconnoitering a prospective battlefield*]: Watch!

[*He walks over to the blackboard and rips it from the wall, where it had been attached by screws. He throws it to the floor*.]

STEEL: Oh!

PAPA: Oh!!

SULTAN: Wow!

[ALIGARI *walks over to the punching bag and rips it off its support, throws it to the floor.*]

STEEL: Yes!

[STEEL *walks over and kicks the punching bag.*]

SULTAN: Wow!

[SULTAN *kicks the punching bag.* PAPA *wordlessly stomps on the blackboard.*

[*Siren noise comes from the* LOUDSPEAKER. ALIGARI *picks up the stool by its legs and swings it against the* LOUDSPEAKER *until the* LOUDSPEAKER *is ripped from the wall and crashes to the floor. The siren noise is cut off abruptly by the action.*

[THE MAN OF STEEL, THE SULTAN OF SWAT, *and* PAPA *walk over to the dead* LOUDSPEAKER, *look at it for a few moments, then turn away from it.*]

ALI [*puffing*]: That's what happens.

SULTAN: Wow!

PAPA: That was remarkable.

STEEL: Boy oh boy, you know what you are?

SULTAN [*exuberantly, with a tone of wonder*]: You're a hero, that's what you are.

ALI: No. No, not a hero. I don't think I want to be called a hero or thought of as a hero. By anyone.

SULTAN: No, but that's what you are. You're a *Hero!*

ALI [*after a slight pause*]: No, I'll tell you who's a hero. [*To the* SULTAN OF SWAT.] You, you're a hero. [*The sultan bows his head.*] [*To* PAPA.] You're a hero. [PAPA *bows his head.*] [*To* THE MAN OF STEEL.] You're a hero. [MAN OF STEEL *bows his head.*] You see. You're the heroes.

SULTAN:
STEEL: } [*together, heads bowed*] Yes, we're the heroes.
PAPA:

ALI: I'm just a man. I work at a desk in a candy factory. [*Pause.*] That is, I used to work at a desk in a candy factory.

SULTAN:
STEEL: } [*together, heads bowed*] A candy factory.
PAPA:

[ALIGARI *walks to the door, reaches for the doorknob, drops his hand to his side. He looks around at all the rubble. Then he puts his hand on the doorknob and wrenches the door crashing open. He looks at the open door for a moment. He takes a deep breath.*]

ALI [*leaving*]: I used to work at a candy factory. [*Pause.*] Goodbye, heroes.

Brothers
in Arms

MERRILL DENISON

CHARACTERS

J. ALTRUS BROWNE, *a business man*
DOROTHEA BROWNE, *his wife*
SYD WHITE ⎫
CHARLIE HENDERSON ⎭ *backwoodsmen*

Produced at Hart House Theatre, Toronto, April 1921, with the following cast:

SYD WHITE	Charles Thompson
DOROTHEA BROWNE	Heasell Mitchell
J. ALTRUS BROWNE	Walter Bowles
CHARLIE HENDERSON	Merrill Denison

Scene: A hunting camp in the backwoods.

Time: Dusk of a November evening, 1919.

A room in an abandoned farmhouse used as a hunting camp during the deer season. There is a door and window in the far wall, a double-tiered wall bunk at the left and at the right a shanty stove. There is a bench beneath the window, a couple of upended boxes near the stove. The room is dirty and squalid.

The curtain rises showing DOROTHEA BROWNE, *a romantic young woman, seated on the bench, her chin in her hand, gazing wistfully into the fire. She shifts her pose so that she may watch her husband, who is pacing nervously up and down.*

J. ALTRUS BROWNIE *is a business man with a penchant for efficiency. He served as a Major in the Army Service Corps during the late war and spent a most rigorous time at Sandgate. He looks forward to the next war.*

DOROTHEA [*pleadingly*]: Altrus, dear, won't you sit down. You're so impatient.

BROWNE [*baring his wrist-watch with a click*]: But Dorothea! We've been here half an hour and not a sign of this man who owns the car. [*Viciously.*] We'll miss that train as sure as . . .

DOROTHEA [*impatiently*]: Oh, I know, dear . . . but don't you love it here? [*Rising, with an outflung-arm gesture.*] This simple camp, its rustic charm . . . the great big out-of-doors? [*Goes to* BROWNE *and fondles his arm and lays her head on his shoulder.*] I don't want to go back to Toronto, Altrus. [*Emphatically.*] I'd like to live in a place like this forever.

BROWNE [*with a tired indrawn breath*]: But, my dear, we must go back.

DOROTHEA: Oh, yes, I know, dear. But this is our first trip together since we've been married. Since you came home from France.

BROWNE [*with controlled impatience*]: Dorothea! I've explained to you that we must catch this midnight train. It is most important. If this man who owns the Ford ever turns up.

DOROTHEA: But, dear . . . you can't do any good by walking around like that. Come and sit down beside me on this simple, rough-hewn bench.

BROWNE [*growling*]: I'm all right, thanks.

DOROTHEA [*her chin on her hand, pensively*]: Oh, it's Canada and it's the wilds. Don't you love the wilds?

BROWNE: I do not! Might have known something like this would happen coming up to a God-forsaken hole twenty miles from a railroad. And if that chap doesn't turn up pretty soon . . .

DOROTHEA [*ecstatically*]: I do hope he does. I'm just

dying to see one of those hunters. They must be such big. fine, simple men, living so close to nature all the time.

BROWNE: I'd like to see the one that drove us up. He'd do me.

DOROTHEA: Why, Altrus. he was only a common taxi-driver. I mean one of those coureurs-de-bois. One of those romantic figures we've read of in books about Canada. And we've seen them in the movies.

BROWNE: Taken in California. probably. [*Half to himself.*] If it took us five hours to drive up to the Mac-Dougals' in the daytime. it will take us a good six to get down to that station tonight.

DOROTHEA [*half to herself*]: I remember the hero in the *Land of Summer Snows.* [*To* BROWNE.] It was about Canada. [*To herself.*] A big. strong. silent man. [*To* BROWNE, *ecstatically.*] Oh, didn't you love him?

BROWNE: Unh?

DOROTHEA: Didn't you love him!

BROWNE [*absently, with puckered brows*]: Love who?

DOROTHEA: That big, strong, silent man in the *Land of Summer Snows.*

BROWNE [*deliberately*]: My dear Dorothea! Can't you realize that if we don't catch that train at Kaladar tonight I stand to lose twenty-five thousand dollars?

DOROTHEA: I know. dear. But I did hope we'd see a real Canadian frontiersman before we left.

BROWNE: We've got to see one before we leave. One frontiersman with a Ford.

DORTHEA [*sobbing*]: You never think of anything but your old business.

BROWNE [*going rapidly to her*]: There, there, dear, there. there. I only worry about the business for your sake dear.

DOROTHEA [*dabbing her eyes*]: It's selfish of me . . . but I can't help being a romantic little fool. [*Blubbering lustily.*]

BROWNE: You're not a fool, dearest. Tell me you're not a fool.

DOROTHEA: Oh, but I am. [*Wiping her eyes.*] And

ever since you met Jim MacDougal on the battlefields
and wrote me of him, I've looked forward to coming
here. During those horrible days of the war when you
were at Sandgate, I've looked forward to coming here,
where you would be safe and out of danger and we might
find romance . . . romance in the land of Robert Service and Ralph Connor.

BROWNE: Yes, yes, dear.

DOROTHEA: I have wanted to see one of those noble
men from whom they drew their characters.

> [DOROTHEA *is sitting on the bench,* ALTRUS *kneel-
> ing beside her. Neither of them sees* SYD WHITE *en-
> ter.* SYD *is a backwoodsman. He is wearing an old
> army tunic and a nondescript cap covered with red;
> his trousers are thrust inside a pair of heavy boots.
> He observes the pair on the bench, nods towards
> them and turns to place his gun against the wall. At
> the sound of the gun falling,* DOROTHEA *starts and*
> BROWNE *rises quickly to his feet.*]

DOROTHEA: Oh!

BROWNE [*importantly to* SYD, *who is going on with
his work*]: My name is Browne, Major J. Altrus Browne.
Mr. MacDougal told me that I'd find the man who drove
me up from the station here.

SYD [*mildly interested*]: Oh, he did, eh? [*Looks at
the stove.*] Fire's kinda low, eh? [*Goes to the corner
and gets some wood.*] You couldn't find no wood, I
s'pose, to put on it. We jest rip a board off'n the floor.
[*Going to the stove.*] Saves a feller quite a bit of time.

BROWNE [*trying to impress* SYD]: I received a very
important business communication this morning which
makes it imperative that I return to Toronto tonight.

SYD: Oh, got to go back, eh?

DOROTHEA: And I do wish he would stay longer. But
the Major is a business man, you know. [*She is trying to
fit* SYD *into innumerable roles in fiction.*]

SYD: Oh, he is, eh? [*Filling his pipe.*] Kinda dark in
here. [*Looks around.*] A feller might have a bit of light.
[*Gets up and prowls around.*] They was a lantrun some
place around here with the chimley cracked.

BROWNE [*impatiently and imperiously*]: Never mind the lantern. We'll only be here a few moments, anyway.

SYD [*still searching under the beds*]: Won't do no harm to have a bit of light. [*Finds the lantern and lights it; the globe is so sooty that just a glimmer shows.*] There, kinda helps make the place more cheerful.

BROWNE: Where is the man who drove us up from the station?

SYD [*hanging the lantern and sitting down behind the stove*]: Well, that's kinda hard to say. When was it he druv you up?

BROWNE: Last Tuesday.

DOROTHEA [*helpfully*]: And it rained the whole way. I loved it.

SYD [*politely*]: Kinda wet, eh? [*To* BROWNE.] Last Tuesday? That musta been Charlie druv you up.

BROWNE: It doesn't matter what his name is. What I want to know is when he will be back.

SYD: Charlie it was. Charlie Henderson. That's who it'd be. He ain't here.

BROWNE: Yes! Yes! Yes! But when will he be here?

SYD [*lighting his pipe*]: Well, that's kinda hard to say. The lads went over to Wolf Lake this mornin'.

BROWNE: This Charlie is with them?

DOROTHEA [*to* SYD]: You know, I think your camp is adorable. It's so simple, and direct. So natural. [*With appropriate gestures.*]

SYD [*to* DOROTHEA]: This here place?

DOROTHEA: Yes. Oh! I love it.

BROWNE: Dorothea!

SYD [*observing* BROWNE *walking near the corner by the head of the beds*]: That floor ain't none too good since we've been using it for the stove.

BROWNE: Never mind about me. [*Exasperated.*] When will these men be back from Wolf Lake?

SYD: Well . . . that's kinda hard to say. It's most ten miles over there and the trail ain't none too good. But I figger they ought to be comin' in most any time now.

BROWNE: And this fellow Henderson will be with them?

SYD: No . . . he won't be with them. That is, it ain't likely.

BROWNE: Can't you understand that I have only five hours to catch that midnight train at Kaladar? And that I must find this fellow Henderson to take me down?

DOROTHEA [*to* SYD]: And I simply hate to think of going back so soon.

SYD: Shame you can't stay till the end of the huntin' season. He might kill a deer.

BROWNE: Dorothea! Will you please try and keep quiet. [*To* SYD.] Now, when will Henderson be back? Answer me definitely.

[SYD *is cleaning his gun for several successive speeches. This adds to the hopelessness of* BROWNE'S *position.*]

SYD: Well . . . that's kinda hard to say. He went still-huntin'[1] over back of the big rock . . .

BROWNE [*almost frantic*]: Yes, but you must know when he'll be here. I've got to have him drive down to that train tonight.

SYD: Oh . . . you want him to drive down to catch the midnight?

BROWNE: Yes, yes, yes. When will he be back?

SYD: Well . . . if he went back of the big rock he'd most likely leave about dark . . .

BROWNE: It's been dark half an hour. How long would it take him to get back?

SYD: I figger it'd take him about half an hour if he had a boat.

BROWNE: Half an hour, eh? Should be here, then, soon. [*Thinks.*] Did he have a boat?

SYD: No . . . he didn't have no boat.

BROWNE [*infuriated*]: What in heaven's name are you talking about a boat for, if he didn't have one?

DOROTHEA: Don't be impatient, dear.

SYD: As I was sayin'—if he had a boat . . .

---

[1] Still-hunting: hunting deer from a fixed position.

BROWNE [*screaming with rage*]: But you said he didn't have one.

DOROTHEA [*helpfully*]: But, dear, if he did have a boat.

BROWNE: Dorothea! will you kindly keep quiet and leave this to me? [*To* SYD.] Now, if it's within the range of human possibility, will you tell me when you expect Henderson back here?

SYD [*laying down his gun and doing his best to be explicit*]: Well, I figger it this way. If he had a boat . . .

DOROTHEA [*patiently*]: He means that if he had a . . .

BROWNE [*disgustedly*]: Let's forget about the boat. On foot, how long would it take him to get over here? Don't you realize that he's got to take me to that train? Will he be back in ten minutes? Twenty minutes?

SYD: Well . . . it's kinda hard to say. He mightn't have went back of the big rock at all. He might have picked up a fresh track and followed it west. But that ain't likely because most of the deer's scared off'n this side of the lake.

DOROTHEA: Oh! What scared them?

BROWNE: Dorothea! How many times must I ask you to keep quiet and not interrupt? I must find out when we can get out of here. [*To* SYD.] You feel sure that he went back of the big rock?

SYD: I figger that's most likely where he's went. And if he couldn't have got the loan of a boat . . .

BROWNE: He might have borrowed a boat then?

DOROTHEA [*helpfully*]: Why, yes, dear, he might have *borrowed* a boat.

BROWNE: Is there some place he might have borrowed a boat?

SYD: No . . . there ain't.

DOROTHEA: You see, dear, he couldn't have got a boat anyway.

BROWNE: Good God!

SYD: Ain't no one's got a boat over here except Levi Weeks and he's got his'n up to Buck Lake.

BROWNE [*striding over to* SYD]: Look here, we've established this point. He couldn't have gotten a boat.

SYD: Well . . . I wouldn't go as far as to say that. He might . . .

DOROTHEA: Dear, won't you sit down?

SYD: Yes, you'd best sit down. That floor ain't none too good.

BROWNE: Never mind about me. I can look out for myself all right.

DOROTHEA: But do be careful, dear.

BROWNE: Dorothea! [*To* SYD.] Now let's find out about your friend Charlie.

SYD: He ain't no particular friend of mine. Kind of a brother-in-law, it seems to me. His half-sister Nellie married my stepbrother Aligan. My father's . . .

DOROTHEA: Why, you're related then.

BROWNE: Dorothea! [*Pleadingly.*] Do keep quiet. [*To* SYD.] He could walk back in an hour, couldn't he?

SYD: He might. But it'd depend on whether he got a deer or not. If he got a fawn and it wasn't too much to heft, he'd most likely try and drug it out.

BROWNE: From what I've seen of this country it's likely he never saw a deer.

DOROTHEA: Why, Altrus, they catch lots of wild things in the wilds.

SYD: Well . . . if he didn't get a deer the chancetes is he'd stay in the bush all night.

BROWNE: Do you mean to say that there is a possibility of his not returning at all?

DOROTHEA: We'd have to stay over then, wouldn't we?

SYD [*laughing*]: I figger you would. He often stays out all night when he's still-huntin'. It ain't likely though. Charlie most often gets his deer. He ought to be here most any time now . . . if he's a-comin' at all.

DOROTHEA: I almost hope he doesn't come. You know, this is the first trip we've had together since we've been married. Since Altrus left his battalion.

SYD: You're his woman, eh? Married?

BROWNE: Dorothea, do shut up. Can't you realize

what twenty-five thousand dollars means to us? [*She pouts.*]

SYD [*seriously*]: If you'd really wanted to have gone, you shoulda went this morning.

BROWNE: I didn't know till four o'clock. [*Angrily.*] I should never have come up into this God-forsaken hole at all.

SYD [*mildly remonstrative*]: This place ain't bad. The deer's about scared off what with the Finches running hounds all the year around, but they's still some left.

BROWNE [*disgustedly*]: I'm not talking about the hunting. I'm talking about the distance it is from the railroad.

DOROTHEA: That's why I love it. It's so far from everything.

SYD: Might be another twenty miles and do no harm.

DOROTHEA [*excitedly*]: Oh, Altrus. He loves the wild, virgin country, too. Far, far from civilization . . . and phones . . . and motors.

BROWNE: I'd give a lot to see one, just one, now.

SYD: It's quite a ways from them things, but I figger it's just as well. Keeps folks outa here in the summer. City folks is a kinda bother.

DOROTHEA: I know. They encroach on the freedom of your life.

SYD: They's always tryin' to get a feller to work. One way and another they figger they's doin' a feller a favour to let him work for 'em.

DOROTHEA: I know, you want to be left alone to lead your own simple life.

BROWNE [*who has been walking like a caged lion and has neared the dangerous corner*]: Simple is right. Now look here. I'm going to give Henderson ten minutes more.

SYD: He might be back in ten minutes. If he got a deer and didn't try to drug it out with him. [*Pause.*] And he come by the lower trail. [*Pause.*] And he didn't stop down to the MacDougals' to listen to that there phonograph. I'd figger he'd most like be about . . .

[DOROTHEA *screams and runs over to* ALTRUS, *who has tripped in a hole and is rubbing his ankle, cursing softly to himself.* SYD *makes no change in position.*]

SYD: I told you to keep out of there.

DOROTHEA: Dearest, what have you done? Did you hurt yourself, dear?

BROWNE: My ankle. [*Hobbles.*] It's only a wrench probably.

SYD [*chuckling*]: I kinda figgered you'd do that. You should've sot down. What did you do? Sprained it?

BROWNE [DOROTHEA *has helped him across to the bench, where he sits rubbing the ankle*]: I didn't do anything to it. [*Explodes.*] It was your infernal floor. Holes all over the place, because you're too damn lazy to chop down a tree for firewood.

SYD [*indignantly*]: We hain't got no time to split firewood when we're huntin'.

DOROTHEA: Did you hurt yourself badly, dear? [BROWNE *winces.*] Oh, do hurry and tear up something clean for a bandage. And get some hot water.

SYD [*laughing*]: There ain't no water nearer'n the lake and there ain't nothin' clean here. He ain't hurt bad.

DOROTHEA [*anxiously*]: I hope not.

SYD: Why, he was lucky. One day last week one of the hounds fell down that there hole and broke his leg. We had to shoot him. You'd do best to sit quiet for a while. Have a chew? [*Offering* BROWNE *a plug, which he refuses with a gesture of repugnance.*] To my way of thinkin' there ain't nothin 'side of a good steady chew to quiet a feller's temper.

BROWNE: I'll just sit here and keep my weight off it for a few minutes. If Henderson isn't here in ten minutes, we'll go.

SYD: Have a chew?

BROWNE [*white with rage*]: My God! I'd like to have had you in my battalion for about six months.

[DOROTHEA *rises.*]

SYD: Yes, you was lucky.

BROWNE: I'd teach you a few things if I had you in the army.

SYD: Was you in the war?

DOROTHEA: Oh, yes. Altrus was in the Army Service Corps for over a year. He was a major.

BROWNE: I'd teach you a few things.

SYD: I suppose you might.

BROWNE: I'd give you ten years if you ever said might again.

SYD: Perhaps you might . . . I was in the army.

DOROTHEA [*with dawning wonderment*]: Dear, he, too, fought for his country in the Great War. You're brothers in arms.

BROWNE [*silencing her with a gesture*]: What outfit were you ever with?

SYD: The 284th Battalion, but I didn't see no sense to it, so I left.

DOROTHEA: How could you leave? Altrus had a lot of trouble getting out. They were awfully mean about it.

BROWNE: Left? Do you mean you deserted?

SYD: No, I didn't desert. The head lads told me to come home. I couldn't get the hang of it like the rest of the lads. They were willin' to walk around doing nothin', but they wasn't no sense to it to my way of thinkin'.

DOROTHEA [*reminiscently*]: I felt that sometimes. [*To* BROWNE.] Didn't you, dear?

BROWNE [*explosively*]: Certainly not. [*To* SYD.] Why, the very thing you need is a few years in the army. Straighten you up, teach you discipline, make a man of you.

DOROTHEA [*to* BROWNE, *brightly*]: It helped you a lot, didn't it, dear? [*To* SYD.] It really was wonderful what the army could do.

SYD: To my way of thinkin' it didn't do nothin' except help make a feller lazy. That's why I couldn't see no sense in it. If they'd been somethun useful for a feller to do I'da stayed and helped them with their war, but they wasn't except in the clink.[2]

[2] Clink: guardhouse or jail. Originally the name of a prison in Southwark.

DOROTHEA: Well, why didn't you get them to transfer you to the Clink Department, if you liked it and were useful there? Altrus got transferred to the Quartermaster's Branch. One is always so much more useful in work one likes.

BROWNE [*looking helplessly at his wife*]: I suppose you spent most of your time in the clink?

SYD: No, not most of it. But a feller was doin' somethun useful there. When I wasn't in jail . . .

DOROTHEA: Oh, who put you in jail?

SYD: One of them head lads. When I wasn't there we done nothin' but drill. One of them head lads'd get us out and walk us. 'Twern't no sense to that. Walkin' a feller around just for the sake of walkin'.

DOROTHEA: It does sound silly, doesn't it, dear?

BROWNE: Dorothea! You know nothing about this at all. [*To* SYD.] Didn't you want to fight for your country?

SYD: To my way of thinkin', that's why I joint the army. But we wasn't doin' no fightin'. We wasn't doin' nothin' but follerin' them head lads around drillin'.

BROWNE: You had to be drilled. You had to learn the rudiments of soldiering.

DOROTHEA: But don't you think they overdid it, now and then, dear?

SYD: To my way of thinkin', they did. Why, them head lads'd make us clean our boots and then walk us around in the dust. Why didn't they keep us inside if they wanted our shoes shiny?

DOROTHEA: I remember all those clean-limbed young fellows at Camp Dix[3] walking along the dusty roads. It did seem a shame. [*To* BROWNE.] You had a horse, didn't you, dear?

BROWNE: Dorothea! [*To* SYD.] But can't you understand that you had to learn the job of soldiering? Your job was to fight Germans and you had to learn how to do it.

SYD [*emphatically*]: That's just what I figgered. All

[3] Camp Dix: In the First World War, Camp Dix was a military camp at Wrightstown, New Jersey. It is now called Fort Dix.

them Germans havin' to be licked and us wastin' our time follerin' them head lads around. They even tried to learn me how to use a gun.

DOROTHEA: How absurd. They didn't really, did they? They wouldn't try to teach a frontiersman to use a gun, would they, dear?

BROWNE: Certainly they would. All these things are very necessary from the standpoint of discipline, my dear.

SYD: That's what the head lads used to say. [*Looking at* BROWNE.] Was you a head lad in the war?

BROWNE: I was an officer.

DOROTHEA [*proudly*]: Oh, yes, my husband was a major and he was much too valuable to go to the front. They kept him, quite against his own wishes, in Sandgate, all during the war, didn't they, Altrus?

BROWNE: Dorothea! Don't be absurd.

DOROTHEA: But you told me so yourself, dear.

SYD: I kinda figgered you was a head lad.

BROWNE [*sarcastically, evasively*]: I suppose you told your officers what you thought of discipline?

SYD: Yes, I says to the head lad, I says, I wasn't goin' to waste my time doin' things they wasn't no sense in.

DOROTHEA: How courageous.

BROWNE [*dumbfounded*]: You told one of your officers that?

SYD [*surprised*]: Yes, I says to him, I says . . .

BROWNE: You were put under arrest, of course.

DOROTHEA: Would they arrest a man just for saying what he thought?

BROWNE: They generally shot them for that.

DOROTHEA [*with enthusiasm*]: But dear, don't you love his sturdy independence? It's so Canadian.

BROWNE: That's not independence. It's insurbordination. What crime did you commit to get you in the guardhouse?

SYD: 'Tweren't no crime.

BROWNE [*sharply*]: But, man alive, you must have done something.

SYD: 'Tweren't no crime. I was out walkin' with my

gun outside the tents where the lads slept and one of the
head lads come around and ast me a lot of questions
which I didn't know the answers for, because they was
kinda riddles anyways, and he got mad and says to me I
was guardin' the camp from Germans.

BROWNE: Why, you were on sentry duty and he was
the officer of the day!

DOROTHEA: But, dear, he said it was at night.

SYD: Yes, it was at night. So I says to him, I says, all
right, just to get rid of him, for I seen they wasn't no
sense to it. They wasn't a German this side of the ocean
and they wasn't no sense hangin' around in the cold. So
I went in and went to bed.

BROWNE [*horrified*]: You could have been shot for
that. On sentry duty and deserted your post.

SYD: That's what the head lad says the next mornin'.
Couldn't shoot a feller fer that. Wouldn't be no sense to
it. I told the head lad, and he seen I was right. He come
near to cryin' and says I could be his batman. But I
·wasn't going to stay up till four in the mornin' to pull
anybody's boots off'n them, let alone one of them head
lads, so he sent me to jail.

DOROTHEA [*romantically*]: How cramping it must
have been to a free out-of-doors spirit like yours. What
did you do?

SYD: I liked it right well, but the head lads wouldn't
let me stay when they found I was kinda enjoyin' it.

BROWNE: My heart bleeds for your officers.

SYD: Them head lads? Why, they didn't do nothin'
but think up ways for us to waste our time.

DOROTHEA: You fought in France, of course? [*With
a change of mood.*] Altrus always wanted to go to the
front and fight, but they wouldn't let him leave England.
I don't know what they would have done without him.
He's so clever at business, you know.

SYD [*genuinely interested*]: He is, eh?

BROWNE [*the conversation is becoming embarrassing*]:
How about this man, Charlie?

SYD: Well . . . he'd been here long ago if he coulda
got a boat.

BROWNE [*he whimpers*]: Back to the navy again?

DOROTHEA: But didn't you adore England? Oh, I love London.

SYD: London's quite a place, but to my way of thinkin' a feller can have just as good a time down here to Belleville.

DOROTHEA [*understandingly*]: I know. You love the simplicity of this big free land.

BROWNE: Too simple-minded to like anything else. How did they get rid of you? Dishonourable discharge?

SYD: No, they wasn't nothin' dishonourable about it. They had a meetin' one day and I told 'em what they ought to do to my way of thinkin', and one of the old fellers, the head lad hisself, I figger it was, says I was incorr . . . incorr . . . incorr . . .

DOROTHEA: Incorruptible.

BROWNE [*explosively*]: Incorruptible nothing. Incorrigible.

SYD: That's it. Says I was goin' home in disgrace. Ain't that just like the army? Why, when I got outside, the rest of the lads says I was a lucky stiff to be gettin' home at all. [*Gets up and listens.*] Someone's comin'.

BROWNE: I can hear no one.

SYD: Perhaps you ain't used to listenin' much in your business. We got a feller up here that got his eyes blew out in France can hear most a mile.

DOROTHEA: Someone is coming, Altrus. I can hear them. Listen! I do hope it's one of those men I've read about.

BROWNE [*peremptorily*]: Is that Henderson? [SYD *nods his head.*]

DOROTHEA: Only the taxi-man. I'm so disappointed.

BROWNE: Well, I'm not. Now we can get something accomplished.

[*He rises, awaiting* CHARLIE's *entrance, as if all would now be well.* SYD *rises and waits expectantly, showing an entirely new interest in life.* DOROTHEA *pettishly fingers a glove.* CHARLIE *comes in the door, carrying a gun, nods to* BROWNE *and his wife, and goes to the stove and warms his hands.*]

CHARLIE: Evenin'. Harye, Syd?

SYD: Any luck?

BROWNE: See here, you're the man who drove us up from the station, aren't you?

CHARLIE: Last Tuesday, wasn't it? [*Turns to* SYD *as if he had no further interest in* BROWNE.] Well, Syd, I got a nice four-year-old buck.

DOROTHEA: Oh, did you catch a buck?

BROWNE: See here, I've got to catch the midnight at Kaladar.

CHARLIE [*politely interested*]: Got to catch the midnight, eh? You'd best be startin' soon.

SYD: Where'd you get him?

CHARLIE: In them hardwoods north of Dyer Lake.

DOROTHEA [*thrilled*]: I'd love to have been there, wouldn't you, dear?

BROWNE: I would not. See here, Henderson!

SYD: How'd you get him, runnin'?

CHARLIE [*sitting down*]: It was this way, Syd. About four o'clock I was about a mile north of Dyer Lake, a-standin' on top of a little rise, smokin'.

DOROTHEA: Isn't it exciting? I do wish we could have been there, don't you, dear?

BROWNE: Dorothea!

CHARLIE: I thought I seen somethin' move, but you know how you can look at a frozen deer and think it ain't nothin' but a tree.

DOROTHEA: Oh, do they freeze?

SYD: It ain't freezin' like ice. They stand still without movin' a hair. Just like that doe I missed yesterday.

BROWNE: Look here, Henderson. I stand to lose twenty-five thousand dollars . . .

CHARLIE: Twenty-five thousand dollars. Quite a lot of money. Just like that doe, it was, Syd. I looked again and seen him move his head. Why, he wasn't seventy-five feet from me.

DOROTHEA [*excitedly*]: Weren't you awfully nervous? I know I would have been. I'm so excited.

SYD [*sucking on his pipe*]: Afraid of scarin' him, eh?

CHARLIE: Yes. Well, I started to drug the rifle to me. Slow . . . slow . . . slow.

BROWNE: Drug it faster, in heaven's name. Shoot your blithering deer and listen to me.

SYD: But you got him, eh?

DOROTHEA: You got him?

CHARLIE: Yes, sir, I got him. I waits for him to move a bit so's I could get a sight on his shoulder. Didn't want to shoot him in the head.

DOROTHEA [*breathless*]: No, you wouldn't want to do that.

CHARLIE: Well. I waited till his shoulder come across the sights and then I took a long breath and drug down on the trigger.

DOROTHEA *and* SYD: What happened?

CHARLIE: I shot him.

DOROTHEA: Did you kill it?

CHARLIE: Dead.

SYD: What did you do with him? Leave him in the bush?

CHARLIE: Cleaned him out and hung him up on a tree.

SYD: Quite a ways in, I suppose?

CHARLIE: No, he ain't very far from the big lake.

SYD [*nodding his head and sucking his pipe*]: He ain't far from the lake, eh? Now Charlie, if you'd only had a boat . . .

[*The dialogue has worked* BROWNE *into a fine frenzy, and at the mention of the boat his control breaks down completely.*]

BROWNE: Oh, God! Let's get out of here. Dorothea, come on.

[*He picks up his coat and stick and marches out of the door,* CHARLIE *and* SYD *rise, very surprised, and* SYD *takes down the lantern.*]

SYD [*leaning out of the door*]: That's a hard trail to follow in the dark. Best take the lantrun.

BROWNE [*outside*]: I don't want your damned lantrun. Come on, Dorothea, we'll go back to the Mac-Dougals'.

[DOROTHEA *goes to the door and waits.*]

CHARLIE: What's the matter with the old feller? Seems kinda crabbed.

SYD [*tersely*]: He was a head lad in the war.

CHARLIE [*understandingly*]: So that's what's the matter with him?

BROWNE [*from some distance*]: Dorothea!

DOROTHEA: Yes, dear. [*To* CHARLIE.] Good-bye, I'm so sorry I have to go, but I have enjoyed your story so much.

BROWNE: Dorothea!

DOROTHEA [*to* SYD]: And I did love your simple, beautiful camp. [*Calling.*] I'm coming, dear.

[DOROTHEA *goes, and* CHARLIE *looks around for wood.*]

CHARLIE: Seems a nice sort of woman.

SYD: About the pure hog's fat, I'd figger. They's some wood over there where Jim ties his hound. [CHARLIE *goes to the corner.*] The old lad fell down the hole a ways back.

[*The two men laugh heartily and* CHARLIE *carries a stick or two over to the stove, puts it in, and then turns questioningly to* SYD.]

CHARLIE: He wasn't thinkin' of going down to Kaladar, tonight?

SYD: Seemed kinda sot on it. Said he wanted you to take him down.

CHARLIE: I wouldn't go down for twenty dollars. Why don't you take him, you ain't doin' nothin'?

SYD: Talked like he wanted you, all the time.

CHARLIE: Don't see why you shouldn't take him. I'll call him. [*Going to the door.*] Hey! Hey! Hey! Back here!

BROWNE [*from some distance*]: What is it?

CHARLIE: Come on back! [*To* SYD.] The chancetes is he might let you drive him in.

SYD: It's kinda hard to say. He seemed sot on havin' you.

[*The two men smoke, waiting for* BROWNE, *who comes in shortly in a very black mood.*]

BROWNE: Well, what is it now?

CHARLIE: We been thinkin'.

BROWNE [*wheeling*]: No! it's impossible.

CHARLIE: No, it ain't impossible. We was wonderin' why you was so all-fired anxious for me to drive you down?

BROWNE: Anybody will do. They told me at the MacDougals' that you were the only person who owned a car.

CHARLIE: Shucks. Syd owns half as much of the car as I do. Why don't you get him to drive you down?

BROWNE: Syd? Syd? Syd who?

CHARLIE: Why, Syd, there. You been talkin' to him for the best part of an hour.

[DOROTHEA *comes in the door.*]

BROWNE: Him?

CHARLIE: Yes, him. Might as well drive the old lad in, Syd. You ain't got nothin' much to do.

SYD [*reaching for his coat*]: No, I ain't got nothin' to do. Might as well a started an hour ago. Been well on the way.

BROWNE: And you stayed here talking when you could have started with us?

SYD: Yes. [*Stopping with one sleeve on.*]

BROWNE [*his temper shot completely*]: Why didn't you say you could drive us in? Why didn't you say you owned half the car? Why did you keep us here wasting valuable time?

SYD: I didn't keep you. I'da taken you in if you'd ast me to.

BROWNE: Well, why in hell didn't you?

SYD: You never ast me.

CHARLIE: No, you never ast him.

DOROTHEA [*helpful to the last*]: Why no, dear. You never asked him once.

[*Curtain.*]

Cobbler,
Stick to
Thy Last

KAY HILL

Cast

STANDFAST BILLINGS, *a cobbler*
FAITHFUL BILLINGS, *his wife*
CHARITY, *a neighbour*
TOM PEPPER, *a young man*
SUSANNA COMFORT, *a young girl*

Place: *The frontier home of* STANDFAST BILLINGS *near Fort Cumberland, Nova Scotia.*

Time: *A day in late fall, about 1780.*

Scene: *The home of* STANDFAST BILLINGS. *The stage is divided by a door or curtain into a bedroom, furnished chiefly with bed, and the living area, roughly furnished with a table, cobbler's bench and tools, a bench and chairs around a table. Trees are visible through a window and a door opening into the yard. It is late fall.*

At rise of curtain: It is morning. In bedroom, CHARITY *is just removing breakfast tray from* FAITHFUL's *lap.* FAITHFUL *waves it away weakly, sinks back on her pillows.* STANDFAST *looks in from living area anxiously. As* CHARITY *passes out with tray, he tiptoes in and goes to his work bench, puts on his apron slowly.* CHARITY *has set down the tray. Now she takes her cloak down from a peg on the wall.*

CHARITY: I mum be off t'farm now, Standfast.

STANDFAST [*heavily*]: Thank'ee, Charity. Tha'rt a good neighbor.

CHARITY [*cheerfully*]: Nay, don't grieve, man, she's mending.

STANDFAST [*not taking this in*]: Twelve years we've been wed—

CHARITY: I tell thee, lad, she's better.

STANDFAST [*pause, puzzled*]: Better? [*Sudden shout, aghast.*] *Better!*

CHARITY: By op in day or so. [*Points to empty tray.*] Appetite's a sure sign.

STANDFAST [*going to look at tray in disbelief; with strong feeling*]: Lord! A man daren't count on owt!

CHARITY: Why, Standfast Billings! Tha wants thy wife to get well, surely!

STANDFAST: Oh, aye! [*Miserably.*] Nobbut when tha've expected the oother—

CHARITY [*with a secret smile*]: Tha moost face oop, Standfast.

STANDFAST [*groaning*]: Eeeh, Charity, if tha knew—

CHARITY [*laughing*]: Nay, but I do, lad!

STANDFAST: Tha know? . . .

CHARITY: About notice to be posted at Halifax: "To any healthy female who'll come to Fort Cumberland to marry Standfast . . ."

STANDFAST [*horrified and alarmed*]: Hold tha noise, woman!

CHARITY [*lower*]: ". . . Standfast Billings, a respectable cobbler aged forty-five, sober, industrious— would make a kind and dutiful husband for any wife." [*She opens the door to go. Furious,* STANDFAST *reaches her, slams it shut again and grabs her arm.*]

STANDFAST: That damned Tom Pepper told thee!

CHARITY: Mind thy manners! [*Frees her arm.*] Aye, the lad coom to me to write down what tha said—so he could post it up on Bulletin Board at Halifax.

STANDFAST [*anxiously*]: Tha never told Faithful?

CHARITY: Nay, but she's bound to find out when lad cooms with thy new wife. [*Laughs.*] Eigh, Standfast, tha ought to've lived up to thy name—and waited a bit!

STANDFAST [*miserably*]: Tha knows there's no woman of marrying age in township. I'd no time to court aboot country for new wife. A cobbler mun stick to his last.

CHARITY: Aye, and to his last *wife* while she lives! Tha might've advertised for housekeeper surely?

STANDFAST [*dismally*]: What woman would coom all the way from Halifax by cart and ship to Partridge Island, and on foot three days through forest—to be housekeeper?

CHARITY: I see tha were fair capped, lad, but tha's stepped from skillet to fire! Tom'll be here any day now with the oother.

STANDFAST: Happen he'll not have found—

CHARITY: I hear they're fair thruss up with single women in Halifax!

STANDFAST [*groaning*]: Then he mun take her back.

CHARITY: Nay, tha know this was his last trip till Spring.

STANDFAST: Charity, can't tha help me?

CHARITY: If tha'd asked, I'd have told thee what ailed thy wife was common enow for her time of life, and wi' right medicine she'd mend.

STANDFAST [*indignantly*]: Tha told me she weren't far from her Maker!

CHARITY [*piously*]: None of us are, Standfast, as t'Good Book tells us. I hoped tha'd see for thyself she just wanted jollying over her bad time and then— [*There is a sudden halloo from outside.* CHARITY *and* STANDFAST *jostle each other in the rush to the window to see. In the bedroom,* FAITHFUL *stirs, moves restlessly.*]

CHARITY: It's Tom!

STANDFAST [*aghast*]: So soon?

CHARITY: And he's got a lass with him!

STANDFAST: Lord! Quick, woman, off with thy cloak—back to bedroom! We daren't let Faithful know. Talk to her—sing to her—owt to keep her from hearing!

CHARITY [*removing cloak*]: Tha'rt only putting trouble off, but I'll do what I can. [*She goes into bedroom just as a knock is heard at the door.*]

FAITHFUL: Who's at door?

CHARITY: Never mind, luv, Standfast will see to it. [CHARITY *fusses over her, fluffing up pillows and so on, while outside* STANDFAST *is struggling to get his apron off.*]

TOM [*off*]: Mr. Billings—it's me, Tom!

STANDFAST: Aye—hold on—I'm cooming!

[*He opens door a crack and* TOM *tries to come in.*]

TOM: Mornin', Mr. Billings. I— [*To his astonishment,* STANDFAST *yanks him inside and closes door.*]

STANDFAST: Coom in, but keep thy voice down!

TOM: But the girl—she—

STANDFAST: She mun wait!

TOM [*proudly*]: I got her—I got your new bride, Mr. Bill—

STANDFAST [*covering* TOM's *mouth with his hand*]: Not so *loud!*

[FAITHFUL *has been struggling to sit up, to listen.* CHARITY *tries to ease her back, soothing her in a low tone.*]

FAITHFUL: Bride? Is some'un getting wed? [STAND-FAST *has drawn* TOM *off to the far corner of the living area, where* TOM *is telling how he found* SUSANNA.]

CHARITY: Nay, tha mun sleep, lass. Tell thee what— I'll sing to thee! [*She sings "The Famous Flower of Serving Men," but any ballad of the period will do, so long as* CHARITY's *own lines can be inserted.*]

Yon beauteous ladies, great and small,
I tell unto you one and all
Whereby that you may understand
What I have suffered in this land—

[*Her voice can drop almost altogether as the others begin to speak normally. Here is another verse, if needed.*]

I was by birth a lady fair,
My father's chief and only heir,

But when my good old father died
Then was I made a young knight's bride.

[TOM *has been glancing, puzzled, toward sound of singing.*]

STANDFAST: Neighbor woman! Fond of singing!

TOM: Oh. Well, that's how it was, sir. Susanna thought it over for a bit and decided to risk it. And there she is, out in the cold——

STANDFAST: Quiet, lad!

TOM: She'll freeze if you don't let her in.

STANDFAST [*glancing toward bedroom*]: I mun think what to do.

TOM [*taking off his hat suddenly and assuming attitude of sympathy*]: Sorry. I forgot. House o' mournin'.

STANDFAST: Tom——

TOM: I hope, sir, as the lady passed over easy.

STANDFAST: She didn't pass——

TOM: She's better off in Heaven, out of this world's misery an' pain——

STANDFAST: Tom, listen——

TOM:——like my Ma said when she died, praisin' God with her last breath, like the Christian woman she——

STANDFAST [*forcefully*]: Tom Pepper, wilt tha shut up and listen!

TOM: Why, sure, Mr. Billings.

STANDFAST: The lass mun be sent back.

TOM [*after a pause, indignantly*]: But you ain't even seen her!

STANDFAST: That's nowt to do with——

CHARITY [*singing louder as their voices rise*]:

Upon the lute sweet William played
And to the same he sung and said——

TOM: She's right smart for a girl——near as smart as my dog!

STANDFAST: I don't want her——

TOM: But you ain't even——

STANDFAST [*voice rising again*]: I don't *need* her now!

CHARITY [*singing, warningly*]:

But all my friends are from me fled
(Now don't forget, your wife's in bed!)

TOM: But you told me yourself. sir— [*Lowering his tone as* STANDFAST *makes frantic shushing motions.*] with your poor wife dead—

STANDFAST [*loud whisper*]: She's not dead!

TOM: Not— [*Mimicking whisper.*] dead?

STANDFAST [*normally, but low*]: She's better. She'll be oop in day or so.

TOM [*pause*]: My soul an' body!

STANDFAST: Nay, I were too hasty, lad, thinking this were my last chance before Spring.

TOM: This is a fine hoot an' holler!

STANDFAST: Tha must tell t'girl, Tom.

TOM: Who, me? Not me!

STANDFAST: But tha can explain—

TOM: Not by a jugful! I ain't used to womenfolk, Mr. Billings. My Ma was the only woman I ever knowed and I was never one to talk back to her. You'll have to tell Susanna yourself—

STANDFAST [*holding* TOM *back as he starts toward door*]: Nay—*how* am I to tell the poor lass—when she's coom all this way—

TOM: That's right! Walked the whole way, never made no complaint. never looked for Injuns behind every tree—an' 'round the campfire at night she'd tell me stories. She used every cent she had buying clothes an' such, and give up a good job at the Great Pontack—an' *I* ain't goin' to be the one to tell her it's all been for nothin'.

STANDFAST: But you being official, Tom, it'd come better from thee!

TOM: No, sir! This don't come under Post Office business.

CHARITY [*singing louder as* FAITHFUL *grows restless*]:

And I myself a lady gay
(Be quick, my man, or hell's to pay)

FAITHFUL [*calling*]: Standfast? . . .
CHARITY [*singing*]:

No braver lady lived, without a doubt,
(My voice, m'lad, is giving out!)

STANDFAST [*calling back*]: A minute now, Faithful, luv! [*To* TOM.] If I moost, then I moost! But I'll tell her outside.
CHARITY [*singing dying down*]:

I had my virgins fair and free
Continually to wait on me—

TOM: It's freezin' out. Poor Susanna—
STANDFAST [*groaning*]: Aye, then, bring her in—but wait till I call thee.

[TOM *nods and leaves.* STANDFAST *hurries to bedroom.*] Only Tom Pepper, luv!

FAITHFUL: Oh. Did he bring any letters?
STANDFAST: Nay, not *letters!* He's gone, but he'll be back—
FAITHFUL: Whatever for, then?
STANDFAST: Why, er—um—to measure for boots!
FAITHFUL [*relaxing*]: Aye—boots. [*As* STANDFAST *moves away.*] Tha'd best go too, Charity. I've Standfast if I need owt.
CHARITY: I'd best sing thee to sleep first—
FAITHFUL [*too quickly*]: Nay! [*Explaining.*] Tha've a good voice, lass, but one can have too much of a good thing. Tha can sing at my funeral, if tha like.
CHARITY [*tucking her in*]: Tha'll not die yet.
FAITHFUL: Soft talk!
CHARITY: Nay, tha'll feel stronger t'morn.
FAITHFUL [*sighing*]: I'll not set foot to floor again, I know that. I'm only waiting for the Lord's hand to grasp mine. [CHARITY *pats her hand, goes out, motioning* STANDFAST *to follow. She puts on her cloak again.*]

STANDFAST [*pleadingly*]: Charity, wilt tha take the lass off my hands?

CHARITY: Nay! I've got a house bulging now with thy bairns— [*Seeing his miserable face, she relents.*] Well—I'll keep her overnight, no longer.

STANDFAST: Thank'ee, lass!

> [STANDFAST *sees* CHARITY *out and beckons to* TOM, *who enters with* SUSANNA, *shivering and looking generally miserable and frightened.* TOM *sets down her bundle inside.*]

TOM: Can I bring Polly in?

STANDFAST [*horrified*]: What! Another?

TOM: My dog, sir.

STANDFAST [*relieved*]: Oh. Nay, tha'll not be staying long.

TOM [*speaking through open crack of door*]: Stay then, Polly. Good girl. [*Closes door. There is a pause while they all look at each other. Then* TOM *speaks uneasily.*] Susanna, this here's Mr. Standfast Billings. [*Turns and makes for the door thankfully.*] Well, I got to be off—

STANDFAST: Don't go, lad!

SUSANNA [*simultaneously*]: Don't leave me, Tom!

TOM [*hesitating*]: But the soljers, up to the Fort—

STANDFAST: They can bide a bit—

SUSANNA [*at the same time*]: Please, Tom, not yet!

TOM [*returning reluctantly*]: I done my part.

STANDFAST: More's the pity!

TOM: 'Twasn't no fault of mine!

STANDFAST: Nay, but— [*grabbing him as he starts for door again.*] Hold on!

SUSANNA [*at the same time, grabbing his other arm*]: No, Tom!

STANDFAST [*pleadingly*]: As a favor—

SUSANNA [*same time*]: Please, Tom!

TOM [*unhappily*]: Well—just for a bit. [*Makes a face at* STANDFAST *behind* SUSANNA'S *back, meaning, "Get on with it!"*]

STANDFAST [*clearing throat*]: Er—ah—coom to fire, lass—tha'rt shivering—

COBBLER, STICK TO THY LAST

SUSANNA [*sticking close to* TOM]: I'm fine here.

STANDFAST [*after a pause*]: Tha must be tired. 'Tis a long way from Halifax.

TOM [*with meaning*]: And a long way back.

SUSANNA [*looking at* TOM]: Back?

STANDFAST: Tha'd better sit down, lass!

SUSANNA [*backing closer to* TOM]: Thank ye, but I'll bide here.

TOM [*after a long pause*]: If somebody don't say somethin' soon— [*Makes threatening move to door.*]

SUSANNA: No, Tom!

STANDFAST: Tha can't go till I've told her!

SUSANNA: Told me what?

STANDFAST [*deep breath*]: Eeeh—the fact is, Susanna, there's been a mistake. I can't marry thee! [*In the bedroom,* FAITHFUL *sits up with a jerk, wide-awake and staring wide-eyed into space.*]

SUSANNA [*hurt*]: I'm honest and healthy. You didn't say I had to be pretty or rich!

STANDFAST: Nay, I'm not complaining. Tha'rt bonny enough— [FAITHFUL, *straining to listen, hears this and throws back the covers.*] Tha would suit me fine in the ordinary way, only—only—

SUSANNA: Only what? [*To* TOM.] For mercy's sake, Tom, what is it?

TOM [*resignedly*]: His wife never died after all. [*Indignantly,* FAITHFUL *leaps out of bed, staggers to the door, stops to listen.*]

SUSANNA: Wife!

STANDFAST: She were sick. I were at my wits' end what to do, with the bairns and all—

SUSANNA: Bairns!

STANDFAST: Six motherless bairns!

SUSANNA: Six!

STANDFAST: Youngest three, oldest ten. I couldn't expect t'neighbors to go on caring for them. I had to have someone, don't tha see, as my wife—uh—

SUSANNA [*indignantly*]: Only she didn't! You brought me all this way—four days through the forest— [*Pause.*] What does your *wife* think?

TOM: She doesn't know yet.

SUSANNA: Why didn't you say you had a wife already!

STANDFAST: I didn't know for how long.

SUSANNA: And six children!

STANDFAST: Tha'd have grown fond of them in time—

SUSANNA: I want children of my own!

STANDFAST: Eigh then, I'm still young! In time tha'd have—um—

SUSANNA [*turning on* TOM]: You're responsible!

TOM [*starting back, amazed*]: Who? Me?

SUSANNA: You posted that notice. You was the one said what a nice man he was!

TOM: But—but—

SUSANNA: You kept quiet about his wife and six children!

TOM: He said to!

SUSANNA [*triumphantly*]: Ah-hah!

STANDFAST: I'm that sorry, lass—but I were desperate.

SUSANNA [*ignoring* STANDFAST, *addressing* TOM]: You never told me! You let me come all this way in the cold—let me spend every penny—and never warned me. So you're responsible— [FAITHFUL, *unnoticed, has stepped into the room.*] and *some*body's got to take care of me!

STANDFAST: Tha'll not suffer, lass. I'll—

FAITHFUL [*in awful tone*]: Tha'll *what*, Standfast? [*All react.* SUSANNA *shrieks and clings to* TOM.]

STANDFAST [*sunk*]: Tha heard.

FAITHFUL [*advancing on him*]: Tha'll *what*, Standfast?

STANDFAST [*anxiously*]: Tha shouldn't be oop, luv!

FAITHFUL: Keep tha distance! Past time I was oop, I'd say.

STANDFAST: Tha'll catch thy death!

FAITHFUL: Tha'd like that, wouldn't tha!

STANDFAST: Nay, lass—

FAITHFUL [*turning on* TOM]: And thee, Tom Pepper
—aren't tha ashamed of thyself?

TOM [*hurt*]: Why is everyone picking on me?

FAITHFUL [*turning on* SUSANNA]: And as for thee,
hussy—

SUSANNA: I'm not a—

FAITHFUL: —out of my house! Back where tha
came from!

TOM: But how can she—

FAITHFUL [*backing them toward the door*]: Tha
brought her. Tha take her back!

TOM: Ferry's off—snow's on the way—

FAITHFUL: Take her to Fort, then.

STANDFAST: Fort's full of men, Faithful. [*As she
turns on him, hastily.*] I did hear as how Jake Smithers
was wanting a boy for his cowsheds. Maybe he'd take a
milkmaid instead.

SUSANNA: I never set out to be a milkmaid. I came in
good faith to get married.

FAITHFUL: If tha didn't know it before, Jezebel, the
law don't let a man have two wives!

STANDFAST [*to* TOM]: Take the lass to Charity for
t'night. We'll see what's best to do t'morn.

TOM [*relieved*]: Sure, Mr. Billings. Come on, Susanna.

SUSANNA [*turning at the door*]: I'm not a hussy—
nor a—a—what you said! [*Exits with* TOM. *As the
door closes,* FAITHFUL *turns and looks at her husband.
He shrinks, starts to speak, gives up, looks miserable.*]

FAITHFUL [*after a pause*]: Well! What've tha to say
for thyself?

STANDFAST: Nay, I meant it for best.

FAITHFUL: Best, aye—best for *thee!* [*She sways a
little and he moves to help her, but she holds him off.*]
Keep away!

STANDFAST: Tha shouldn't be oop, lass.

FAITHFUL: Tha were glad to think I'd be dead and
gone, and then tha could wed yon lass. Tha wouldn't
have grieved for me a minute!

STANDFAST: Tha'rt wrong, lass. I were trying to put a

good face on things. The Lord tells us to accept our misfortunes with a cheerful spirit—

FAITHFUL: Cheerful, aye!

STANDFAST: —and do the best I could for the bairns!

FAITHFUL: Burying me before my time—driven by thy lustful haste!

STANDFAST: Not lust! Winter!

FAITHFUL: Tha've been wishing to be rid of me now I'm old—

STANDFAST [*shocked*]: Tha'rt wrong, lass!

FAITHFUL: I bore thy children, took care of thy home, nursed thee in sickness—and see the thanks I get.

STANDFAST: Now, luv—

FAITHFUL: Tha couldn't wait to put some'un in my shoes! The faithless gommick! Tha would-be widower! I'll show thee then! I'll see *thee* off! I'll live till I'm a hundred and make all thy days miserable—and when th'art gone, *I'll* wed again!

STANDFAST [*sadly*]: I don't blame thee for being vexed, lass, but we've had our differences before— [*Moves toward her hopefully.*]

FAITHFUL [*seizing poker and threatening him with it*]: Coom another step and I'll clap thee one!

STANDFAST [*despairingly*]: Eee-ah! [*Getting a little angry.*] What's doon is doon! Still I'll do t'best I can to right matters. [*Taking his hat and coat from a peg.*] I'll talk to Smithers, see if he'll take the lass off our hands.

FAITHFUL: Go then and be quick! [*Anxiously.*] But say she's friend of Tom's—we needn't be laughing-stock of whole township.

STANDFAST [*pausing at the door*]: Wilt tha be all right? Tha should be in bed—

FAITHFUL [*bitterly*]: *Now* tha worry—when I never felt healthier in my life. Be off. [STANDFAST *exits. When door has closed,* FAITHFUL *droops, sways, feels her way to chair, sinks into it, drops her head in her hands, the picture of misery and hurt.*

[*In a moment there's a timid rap at the door.* FAITHFUL *at once stiffens, her face grim. She*

seizes the poker and then opens the door. SUSANNA
stands outside.]

FAITHFUL: What now, tha faithless— [*Stops short as
she sees* SUSANNA.] What! Thee again? T'cheek!

SUSANNA [*nervously*]: Please, ma'am—can I come in?

FAITHFUL: Aye—coom in and shut door—dost want
to kill me with draught? [*Takes wool shawl off table and
wraps it around her shoulders.*] Aye, that's just what tha
want!

SUSANNA: Oh, no, ma'am! I'm—I'm sorry for what
happened—

FAITHFUL: What *didn't* happen, tha mean! Aye, you
thought to get a good husband for thyself—
[*Jealously.*] Did tha talk with him outside now? Is that
why—

SUSANNA: No, ma'am, no. I asked Tom to bring me
back. [*Nervous but determined.*] Mistress Billings, I'll
not be disposed of as though I were a cow or a—

FAITHFUL: If tha had brass in thy pocket, or a way
to get back where tha coom from, tha might have some
say in the matter. Tell me summat. How was it tha
coom to answer Standfast's advertising?

SUSANNA: I came to Halifax from England with my
parents six months ago, ma'am. They died on the voy-
age and I was left alone. I had to take any work I could
get. It was long hours at the Great Pontack and nobody
my own kind to talk to—I was lonely. I wanted to live
in the country, have a home and family—and—and this
seemed a good chance.

FAITHFUL [*softer tone*]: I see. Happen 'tis not all
thy fault. But what's to be done with thee now? If that
gormless Tom hadn't—

SUSANNA: It wasn't Tom's fault!

FAITHFUL: It's mine, tha think—for not dying?

SUSANNA: No, no!

FAITHFUL [*bitterly*]: The tale will be all over township by Spring. A proper fool I'll look. Standfast, too.

SUSANNA: Mistress, it needn't be known.

FAITHFUL: Dost tha think it can be kept quiet with
thee here, a stranger, alone!

SUSANNA: If I could get married—

FAITHFUL: Not to my husband!

SUSANNA: Of course not. He's old enough to be my father.

FAITHFUL: He's yoong enough some ways! Who then? Ah—Tom!

SUSANNA [*shyly*]: We were together all these three days and nights in the woods—

FAITHFUL: Ah-hah!

SUSANNA: It's not what you think! He never laid a hand on me.

FAITHFUL: But tha wanted him to!

SUSANNA: I've taken an awful fancy to him, ma'am.

FAITHFUL [*cheerful all of a sudden*]: Well, lass, why not? He's single. Dost know how *he* feels?

SUSANNA: I think he likes me, but I guess not the way I want him to.

FAITHFUL: And in three days and nights tha couldn't bring him up to mark?

SUSANNA: I tried. The last night, I called him to come and tuck in my blankets. [*Sadly.*] He just tucked them in and went back to sleep with Polly, his dog.

FAITHFUL [*thoughtfully*]: The lad were brought up religious—

SUSANNA: Perhaps he's shy.

FAITHFUL: More gormless than shy, I reckon. His father, a Scots trapper, got killed by Indians soon after the lad was born, and his mother stayed on in forest, settin' t' traps herself and selling t' furs till Tom was grown. She kept the lad close to home, away from evil influences! She were a cold woman—real sharp with the lad from what I hear—gave him nowt but sermons. All the love he ever got was from dogs, and so—

SUSANNA: So that's it! He just don't know about living humans!

FAITHFUL: Happen tha's right, and if so—h'mmm—

SUSANNA [*eagerly*]: If so?

FAITHFUL: If he never had straight talk from his mother—and never saw farm livestock where he lived

—just wild things of the forest—mercy! It's time the lad learned a thing or two!

SUSANNA: Do you think if he did, he'd be more interested in me?

FAITHFUL: Aye! But who's to tell him? [*Hastily.*] Not I. [*Sudden grim smile.*] Standfast!

SUSANNA: But do you think he would?

FAITHFUL [*grimly*]: He'd better! Or I'll make his life that miserable he'd like to be dead. 'Tis only fair, seeing he got thee into this. Jake Smithers' farm wouldn't suit you, lass. His wife's the meanest creature in Nova Scotia and the worst cook in Cumberland County. [*Glancing out window.*] Here comes yon billy-tup o' mine now. Go in bedroom, child, and lay down thy cloak. Take thy gear with thee. [SUSANNA *gathers up her bundles and goes quickly into bedroom, then listens to ensuing conversation.*]

[STANDFAST *enters with an uncertain but hopeful air about him.*]

STANDFAST: I fixed it, Faithful! Jake says he'll be glad to take the lass on his place!

FAITHFUL [*grimly*]: Happen he may, but she'd do better to wed Tom.

STANDFAST [*amazed*]: Wed—Tom? Tom *Pepper?*

FAITHFUL: He's a good lad, and with a wife he'd settle down. Running about with mail's no future.

STANDFAST: Tom wants to wed lass?

FAITHFUL: I don't suppose he'll object once he knows what's in t'wind. But *tha* mun give him boost!

STANDFAST [*eagerly*]: Anything, luv, if tha'll get over being vexed—

FAITHFUL [*sharply*]: I may not feel so bitter if tha dost as I say!

STANDFAST: Just say!

FAITHFUL: Tha mun bring those two together.

STANDFAST: Bring— [*Pause.*] How?

FAITHFUL [*snappily*]: Tha did all right for *thyself!* The truth is, Tom knows nowt of love and wedding and t'like.

STANDFAST [*puzzled*]: Nowt?

FAITHFUL [*with emphasis*]: Nowt. He's never laid wi' a woman!

STANDFAST: Eee-ah! Tha don't say!

FAITHFUL: I don't think that mother of his told him owt. Tha mun find out if I'm right and if so, tha mun tell him.

STANDFAST: Tell him? . . .

FAITHFUL [*impatiently*]: About wedding and getting bairns!

STANDFAST: Oh—aye.

FAITHFUL: And if tha don't do proper job of it, tha'll not see inside of thy bedroom for month of Sundays, not though tha pray on thy knees.

STANDFAST [*starting for the door*]: I'll tell the lad now!

FAITHFUL: Nay! Tha'll do it here! [STANDFAST *stops in mid-step, turns around.*]

STANDFAST: Here?

FAITHFUL: I mun make sure the job's doon, and doon proper. Call him in. That's a decent lass tha brought all the way from Halifax on fool's errand. It's up to thee now to put things right.

STANDFAST [*uneasily*]: Tha'll let me talk to the lad alone?

FAITHFUL: Aye—but I'll be in bedroom. [*Exits to bedroom.*]

STANDFAST [*groaning*]: Oh—Champion! [*Scratches his head.*] Eeee—however will I—

[*The door opens and* TOM *puts his head in.*]

TOM: Is Susanna almost ready?

STANDFAST: Eee—coom in, lad—I were just going to call thee.

TOM [*coming in and closing door, looking around*]: Where—

STANDFAST: In yon—with my wife. Tom, I—I mun have a talk with thee.

TOM: What about? Can't stay long. Soljers waitin' for their letters.

STANDFAST: This won't take long.

TOM [*after a longish pause*]: Mr. Billings?

[STANDFAST, *deep in thought, jumps a little.*]

STANDFAST: Eh?

TOM: Said tha wanted to talk.

STANDFAST: Oh, aye. [*Pause.*] Tom, did tha ever think to get wed?

TOM: Nope.

STANDFAST: Why not then?

TOM: I'm fine as I am.

STANDFAST: Tha mun wed soom day.

TOM: Why?

STANDFAST: All men wed!

TOM: Not all. There's the Captain up to the Fort and most of the men—they ain't married.

STANDFAST: How old art tha?

TOM: Seventeen.

STANDFAST: And tha don't know owt about getting wed!

TOM: Sure, I know!

STANDFAST [*surprised*]: Oh, tha do!

TOM: Preacher talks over you, then you take up a farm and settle down. And pretty soon the bears start bringin' kids.

STANDFAST: Bears!

TOM: That's right. And a feller don't get any peace after that.

STANDFAST: Bears don't bring bairns!

TOM: My mother said they do!

STANDFAST: Faithful's right! Tha don't know owt about owt!

TOM [*indignantly*]: I find a path in the forest as good as an Injun! I can make a fire with only—

STANDFAST [*soothingly*]: Nay, nay—I mean about women!

TOM: Only woman I ever knew was Ma, and she—

STANDFAST: Tha'rt a grown man now, Tom. Tha mun learn about—about wedding and such.

TOM: All right.

STANDFAST: All right—what?

TOM: I'm listening. [STANDFAST *paces nervously, finally stops before* TOM.]

STANDFAST [*solemnly*]: Tom, there's more to wedding a lass than preacher talking over thee. [*Pause.*] There's—there's the going to bed. [*Pause.*] Tha go to bed alone now and it's cold and lonely—

TOM [*cheerfully*]: Not for me it ain't. I curl up with Polly.

STANDFAST: Tha'd find it nicer going to bed with woman, Tom. A woman's soft—and nice—and—

TOM: So's Polly.

STANDFAST: Tha can't compare a dog with a woman!

TOM: Seems to me dogs is better. Dogs don't yell at you or bawl you out. And dogs do what you tell 'em! Yep. dogs got it all over women.

STANDFAST: Forget dogs, wilt tha!

TOM: What's so fussy about women, Mr. Billings?

STANDFAST: Well, they—they're different—from men.

TOM: I can see that.

STANDFAST: There's differences tha can't see!

TOM: Like what?

STANDFAST [*with a glance toward bedroom; bursting out*]: Dammit, man, hast never seen boar with sow?

TOM [*shaking his head*]: We'd no pigs in the forest. [STANDFAST *groans, takes another nervous walk up and down, has another try.*]

STANDFAST: Listen! The Bible says it's not good for t'man to be alone.

TOM: I got Polly.

STANDFAST: Not dogs! The Good Book means men and women! It says "What God hath joined"— [*Demonstrating by locking his fingers together.*] joined, see? Joined *together*! Now dost tha see?

TOM [*mystified*]: Nope. [STANDFAST *takes another walk, stops once more in front of* TOM.]

STANDFAST: Women are better nor dogs any day! Take my word for it!

TOM [*doggedly*]: Every feller to his taste.

STANDFAST: Can a dog cook and clean for thee?

Mind thy bairns? Bring them up to support thee in thy old age?

TOM: A woman can't run down rabbits!

STANDFAST [*angrily*]: Don't tha be making a joke of women! A good woman's worth two of *thee!*

TOM [*abashed*]: Sorry.

STANDFAST: Listen, lad, I've a wife, as thee know— and a wife I wouldn't trade for *ten* dogs!

TOM: Yes, sir. Your wife's all right, I guess, but—

STANDFAST [*indignantly*]: All right? Eeee! There's nowt like her! And tha should taste her puddings! [FAITHFUL, *listening, reacts, first frowning, now beginning to smile a little.*] When I thought I were losing her, I were that desperate I started looking quick for anoother! Summat *too* quick as it turned out—but sithee, Tom, if marriage weren't good, would I want to wed again—even for the sake of bairns?

TOM: But I'm so happy the way I am! I wouldn't mind marryin' so much if it weren't for them bears bringing—

STANDFAST [*violently*]: Just get one thing in thy thick head, wilt tha? Bears don't bring bairns!

TOM [*after a pause*]: Then where do they come from, Mr. Billings?

STANDFAST: From humans!

TOM [*another pause*]: How?

STANDFAST [*gulping*]: How?

TOM [*nodding*]: Where do folks get 'em from?

STANDFAST [*harassed*]: They don't get them from anywhere—they *make* them!

TOM [*startled*]: Honest? [STANDFAST *nods hopefully.*] You're a smart man, Mr. Billings, I know, and well respected, so I guess I should take your word for it. [STANDFAST *beams and nods again.*] But *how* do they make 'em? [STANDFAST *looks glum again.*] What do they make 'em *out* of?

STANDFAST [*looking about wildly*]: They make— [*Pause.*] they make them from—out of— [*Inspiration, his eyes lighting on the Bible.*] out of love!

TOM [*vaguely*]: Love?

STANDFAST [*strongly*]: Aye, lad. Tha wouldn't know about love mayhap. So let me tell thee how it is. The love of woman's a lamp unto her husband's feet—a light in his path. She makes his life sweet, Tom, sweeter also than the honey and the honeycomb. [FAITHFUL, *overwhelmed, furtively wipes away a tear, but* TOM *isn't so affected.*]

TOM: Them are sure nice words—

STANDFAST: They coom from Bible, lad, so they mun be true.

TOM [*carelessly*]: Still, I'd as soon stay single, I guess.

STANDFAST [*throwing up his hands*]: Give oop! Come out, tha two!

[*The two women appear,* SUSANNA *disappointed and angry,* FAITHFUL *softened by love, though* STANDFAST *is not yet aware of it.*]

STANDFAST [*gloomily*]: It put me off, knowing thee two were listening.

TOM [*cheerfully*]: Come on, Susanna. I'll take you to Mistress Charity, and tomorrow you'll—

SUSANNA [*bursting out at him furiously*]: And tomorrow I'm to go to Mrs. Smithers and probably starve to death! *You* don't care!

TOM [*amazed*]: I thought you'd be glad to—

SUSANNA [*stormily*]: You thought—*you* thought! You don't have anything to think *with*, just a lump of solid bone! You don't know a thing except about Injuns and dogs! I wish I'd never set eyes on you—you—you dog-lover! [*She rushes back into the bedroom, mopping away angry tears. Through the following scene, she drearily puts on bonnet and cloak and gathers up her things.*]

TOM [*disgustedly, to* STANDFAST]: Women! Soft and nice! Tell her I'll wait outside. [*Opens door and calls.*] Polly! [*Exits.*] Here, Polly—ah, good girl! Good Polly—that's my girl! [*Puts his head in.*] Give me a dog any day! [*Closes door.* FAITHFUL *goes to stand by* STANDFAST.]

STANDFAST [*helplessly*]: Eee, by gum.

FAITHFUL: Standfast, did tha mean t'things tha said?

STANDFAST [*puzzled*]: Things? What things?

FAITHFUL: About wedding—and love and that.

STANDFAST: Oh, aye. [*Sadly.*] But it weren't enow to do the trick.

FAITHFUL [*putting her hand on his*]: It were enow for me, luv. Why in name of goodness didn't tha ever say such things to *me*?

STANDFAST [*astonished*]: Surely tha knew?

FAITHFUL: Nay, I thought tha took me for granted —like horse and barn.

STANDFAST: That's daft!

FAITHFUL: I know that now, lad.

STANDFAST [*hopefully*]: Tha'rt not vexed any more? [*She smiles and he seizes her joyfully.*] Eeee, luv! I've been that wild these past weeks, what with the thought of losing thee—and worrying about the bairns, to bring them up the way tha'd want!

FAITHFUL [*holding him off as bedroom door opens*]: Nay, lad—not yet! [*Low.*] Go out there now and tell Tom plain facts—

STANDFAST: Aye!

FAITHFUL [*loudly*]: Fetch Tom, Standfast. That gear's too heavy for the lass to carry. [STANDFAST *exits briskly.* SUSANNA *sets down her bundles.*] I'm that sorry, Susanna, the way things turned out—

SUSANNA [*sadly*]: It just wasn't to be.

FAITHFUL: But tha mun keep hoping—

SUSANNA: It's no good. You and Mr. Billings did your best—

[*She stops, turns her back, as* TOM *enters with* STANDFAST: TOM *stumbles over the threshold because he's got his head turned, staring back at* STANDFAST. *His face is shocked.*]

TOM [*flatly*]: I don't believe it!

STANDFAST [*grinning*]: Tha will! [*He winks at* FAITHFUL *and nods.*]

TOM: Honest Injun?

STANDFAST: My hand on t'Bible.

TOM: Lordy! [*He looks at* STANDFAST, *then at* FAITH-

FUL, *then at* SUSANNA. STANDFAST *picks up* SUSANNA's *parcels and loads them on* TOM.]

FAITHFUL: Tha'll be taking her along to Charity's now?

TOM [*pulling himself together with an effort*]: Uh—Sure! I'm ready if she is!

[SUSANNA *marches past him to the door, head in the air.*]

FAITHFUL: Now, Tom—Susanna—tha'll not part in anger, surely. [*She looks hard at* SUSANNA.] Why don't tha kiss and make oop?

TOM [*scowling*]: Kiss *her?*

SUSANNA [*loftily*]: I'd as soon kiss Polly! Sooner.

TOM: Me, too!

FAITHFUL [*warningly*]: It's not likely tha'll see each other again. The Smithers folk aren't much for letter-writing.

SUSSANA [*getting the message*]: Oh! [*Looks at* TOM *uncertainly.*] Maybe—maybe that's right, Tom. [*Moving a little toward him.*] After all. we've been friends for three whole days. I enjoyed the trip. Did you?

TOM [*backing a little*]: Uh-huh.

SUSANNA: And the stories I told around the camp-fire?

TOM: Uh-huh.

SUSANNA [*smiling coaxingly*]: So—just in case we shouldn't meet again—will you kiss me good-by, Tom?

TOM [*panicking*]: Kiss! No! I never—I don't—

SUSANNA: Then I'll kiss you! [*And she does.* TOM *stands stock still, stiff, hands straight at his sides and cumbered with* SUSANNA's *parcels. Just at the end of the kiss, he jerks a little, his hands start to go up, parcels and all, but* SUSANNA *breaks the kiss and steps back, discouraged. She turns to* FAITHFUL.] It's no use! [*Sadly.*] Good-by, Tom. [TOM *is staring blankly into space.*]

FAITHFUL [*watching him*]: Patience, lass!

TOM [*in a high, cracked voice*]: Susanna? [*Repeating in deeper voice.*] Susanna! I got to do that again!

SUSANNA [*eagerly*]: Why, Tom?

TOM: Never mind! [*This time he puts his arms*

around her awkwardly and does at least half the kissing. Then he breaks loose, looks at her as if seeing her for the first time, then grabs her again and kisses her thoroughly, whirls her around in his arms exuberantly.] Whee! By George, Mr. Billings, you never said the half of it!

STANDFAST [*grinning and putting an arm around* FAITHFUL]: Well—by gum—I tried!

TOM [*masterfully*]: Susanna, we're gettin' married!

SUSANNA: Yes, Tom!

TOM: Soon's we can find a preacher! [*Kisses her again.*]

STANDFAST: Eeeah! Tha learns quick, lad!

TOM: It's like you said, Mr. Billings—sweeter'n honey!

STANDFAST [*folding* FAITHFUL *in his arms*]: Tha's dead right!

TOM [*beaming*]: Why—dogs just ain't in it at all!

[*Curtain.*]

Breakdown

WILFRID WERRY

CHARACTERS

MARY BRIDGMAN
JOHN BRIDGMAN
JOHN'S OTHER SELF
MR. BAINARD

Scene: The breakfast room of a moderately priced cottage in the suburbs of a large Canadian city.
   Time: An autumn morning.

The breakfast room is quite plainly furnished. There is a bay window, left, overlooking the yard. Beneath it, a window seat with a hinged top. A low buffet is in a corner of the room. A table, near the centre of the room, is laid for one. There is toast on a plate and an egg in an egg-cup. A door, right, leads to the hallway. There is a telephone on a small stand, just beside the doorway. It is a rather dull, bare room. The weather also is dull.
   MARY BRIDGMAN, *a pleasant, wifely young woman of about thirty-five, is putting the finishing touches to the table. She is dressed simply.*

MARY [*calling*]: Breakfast's on the table, John.
   [*She places a napkin at the side of the plate, fuss-*

ing about the arrangement. She looks up, anxiously, as JOHN BRIDGMAN *enters.* JOHN *is about thirty-nine, pale and tired-looking. His expression is that of a disillusioned man. He sits, or rather, slumps into a chair at the table, and looks at the food without interest.*]

JOHN: Have the children gone?

MARY: A little while ago.

JOHN: It must be getting late, I—

MARY: It's only nine-thirty. I didn't want to disturb you. Get your sleep while you can. You'll need all your strength.

[*As she speaks,* JOHN'S OTHER SELF *appears and stands directly behind* JOHN's *chair. This is the self that is the result of his breakdown. He follows* JOHN *about like an evil twin. His voice is driving and penetrating, though not loud, rather rhythmic in its beat. His clothes are dark, his complexion pale.* MARY *busies herself with tidying up.*]

OTHER SELF: Strength? Why? And sleep. For your work? There's a laugh! Sleep—sleep—if only you *could* sleep. "Sleep that knits up . . ." You can't remember the words. You don't always remember so well now, do you?

JOHN: Yes, I'll need all my strength.

MARY: Did you sleep well?

JOHN: Fine, once I dozed off.

MARY: I didn't hear a thing till the alarm went off.

JOHN [*sharply, as he tops his egg*]: Stop worrying, Mary! I'm cured. Let's forget it!

OTHER SELF: There's a laugh; forget it! Forget—the Rest Home—the long white corridors—the starched white dresses of the nurses—the ascetical white coats of the doctors—white, white, white! And the enveloping blackness! Forget? The soft voices—the soft shoes—and the hard needles in your arm—*forget?*

MARY: It was nice and cool for sleeping. Makes one think of winter, almost.

JOHN [*munching toast*]: Yes. I slept fine after I dozed off, just fine.

OTHER SELF: Dozed off? It was almost dawn then. How many hours did you lie awake, afraid to move for fear Mary would hear? You lie awake—afraid to think—

MARY: You're not eating your egg! Is it done right? You *must* have an egg for breakfast.

JOHN [*phlegmatically tackling the egg*]: I'm—not very hungry this morning. I'll have a good lunch.

OTHER SELF: Only men who work are hungry. You enjoyed breakfast once; breakfast starts the day, as the seed starts the plant. You hate it now! You have to see Mary, perhaps the girls. You have to go to work where there is no work. Start to live a lie again.

MARY [*reflectively*]: You used to have such an enormous appetite in the morning. I was afraid you'd weigh three hundred before you were forty.

OTHER SELF: Forty is approaching—and where are you?

JOHN: I'll do a lot of walking today. I'll be ready for a good supper.

MARY: I was just reading how good walking is for the heart.

OTHER SELF: Yes—you'll do a lot of walking, but you won't get anywhere. You'll drink coffee in some obscure spot—for you've nowhere else to go. And you'll wonder why some of the other men linger over theirs, too. Perhaps they've had to "rest" a while. [*Softly.*] If you were dead, you wouldn't have to play this miserable game.

JOHN [*sitting up straighter*]: You had your breakfast?

MARY: Yes, with the girls. I tried that new cereal. They loved it.

JOHN: It's advertised enough. You'd think they were all going to be giants, after three bowls full. I'm glad they like it.

OTHER SELF: But they can't like their father. He's a shadow, a man who comes and goes but leaves no mark of love upon them.

MARY: The girls are certainly growing. Their dresses . . . [*She pauses in embarrassment.*]

JOHN [*making a stab at levity*]: Soon, we'll have to plan for their college or marriage. I'll have to get cracking.

OTHER SELF: Do you notice the way they look at you? You were away too long—for your "health." And you don't bring them pretty little things like other fathers. How can you?

JOHN [*finishing his egg and attempting to sound busy*]: You should have called me earlier. There's a man I must see.

MARY: I'm sorry. It's not very late; take the car.

OTHER SELF: Late! It's always late—too late or too early. "Next spring. We had something last week. Give us a ring sometime. Feeling better?" In the back of their minds—the Rest Home—

MARY [*at telephone table, picking up pad*]: Oh, dear, I do wish Ruth would learn to write as well as Jane!

JOHN: What is it?

MARY: Some message.

JOHN: For me?

OTHER SELF [*ironically*]: For you? A message?

MARY: I can't make it out. [*Reading, with difficulty.*] A "Mr. Rainyards" telephoned. It couldn't be terribly important; otherwise, he would have phoned back. [*She removes the sheet from the pad; tosses it into the waste-paper basket.*]

JOHN [*rising*]: Yes, I think I'll take the car. I'll get around faster.

MARY: Who're you going to see? [*She pauses, sensing that this is a wrong question.*]

JOHN: A man downtown. We—went to college together. Said to call him anytime. It isn't exactly in my line, but—

OTHER SELF: Pretty good, that one! A man downtown. If there were one, he'd dodge you. Mary knows you're lying.

MARY: You haven't had your coffee!

JOHN: Oh, yes—my coffee. [*He sits again;* MARY *pours the coffee.*]

MARY: Black or *with?*

JOHN: With.

[MARY *leans over.* JOHN *kisses her. They both try to smile.*]

MARY: Just like our first breakfast together! It was so lovely. I never thought I could get used to a man who didn't take cream in his coffee. But when you said with —with a kiss—I didn't seem to mind any more!

OTHER SELF: These are the silly little things that haven't changed.

JOHN: I don't think I'm really awake without black coffee. Habit, I guess.

MARY: Did you see Ed Murkel yesterday?

JOHN: Yes, but you know how busy he is. People bulging out of his front office—all looking for something.

OTHER SELF: Yes, you saw Alderman Murkel. contractor, general liar and crooked front man for a dozen shady enterprises. You couldn't go through that again! He gave you a fat cigar and a glass of the finest Scotch. Then he sat and gloated like a frog that had a fly on a platter.

MARY: I'm glad he didn't have anything for you. It would have been a dirty political job.

OTHER SELF: He saw you, at least. It's the ones who give you the brush-off—

MARY [*crossing with small dish*]: Here's some of my best marmalade. Kept it especially for today—our anniversary! Something nice is going to happen today, I can feel it.

JOHN: Yes, it's a new day. I wonder what it will bring? [*Reflectively.*] Married ten years. Hard to believe, isn't it?

[*They both look quite happy for a moment; then* JOHN *slumps back into his chair again.*]

OTHER SELF: Ten years! Poor Mary. And today will bring another disappointment.

MARY: And I don't regret a single day of it! [*Lightly.*] Have I been a good wife, John?

JOHN: Much too good for me. We should have a party tonight.

MARY: We'll make up for it next year.

OTHER SELF: Instead, tonight, you'll go to bed. To nightmares that leave you sweating, and you'll sit up, ready to scream that you won't go back to the white, blinding corridors and the men who ask questions you cannot answer.

JOHN: Sure, next year. It's a date.

OTHER SELF: Next year—another anniversary—in the Rest Home. Why go on? Why face the custom-tailored suits and the blank faces above them, seated behind their oversized desks? They're afraid of you! You died somewhere among the white corridors and the night screams.

MARY: I'll start planning now! [*Lightly.*] We'll take in the Military Ball. I'll wear a deep blue I saw in Carson's. You'll wear your medals.

JOHN: You could probably buy them for a dollar now.

MARY: Yes, but not earn them.

JOHN: Keep 'em polished bright for the next war! Funny, it wasn't so bad, now I see it clearly—you could only be killed. I'd something to fight, then.

OTHER SELF: Why didn't you fight old Bainard, when he dismissed you? "Necessary changes in personnel—new partner insists—sorry, John!" Cryptic excuses—confusion—mind spinning and whirling! Fight? No, instead, you sank into—quicksand.

MARY [*thinking; then, flaring up a bit*]: Something to fight? You've something to fight now, and a family to fight for! I can't understand you sometimes! Are you *really* fighting for a job?

JOHN: You haven't been out with me—since—since I left the Rest Home. You haven't seen their faces—my old friends'. I saw Harper the other day. He hurried off so quickly he nearly fell into a trash can. He only got my job because I showed him the accounts.

OTHER SELF: He's also brother-in-law of Mr. Bain-

ard, and a pal of the new partner. Make way for rela-
tives!

MARY: And he pretended to be so nice when we had
him out for dinner, remember? Perhaps he could do
something for you. After all, you were their chief accountant.

OTHER SELF: Ah, those are the ones who forget.

JOHN: I can't understand it. And I can't think about
it. I begin thinking in circles.

OTHER SELF: That was the way it started.

MARY: Then start with a new firm. It's the job that
matters. You know your work.

OTHER SELF: It isn't the work. It's the forms: "Your
last job? *Why* did you leave? *Where* have you been confined this last year?"

JOHN: Perhaps I should look up the old boys from
the regiment?

MARY [*proudly*]: And show them Captain Bridgman, M.C., Croix de Guerre, is still a soldier! I was so
proud of you, John; they were, too!

OTHER SELF: Sure, they'll buy you a drink—and discuss the old days. But not jobs. "Haven't seen you for a
while. Been away? See you in the next war!"

MARY: If Jeff and Harry had come through it, they'd
have understood.

OTHER SELF: You used to pity them, your best
friends. They died so young. Now they can pity you.
Their names are on the honour rolls—yours isn't even
on an office door. Soon you won't have a name.

[*The doorbell rings.*]

MARY [*crossing to answer bell*]: Probably the mail.
There may be something. It takes only one letter . . .
[*She disappears.*]

JOHN: Bert Carter promised he'd write.

OTHER SELF: Delusive talk. Bert Carter's too busy
for—

JOHN [*half to himself*]: I wonder how long a man
may be dead without knowing it . . .

[MARY *returns. She has a letter and the newspaper.*

*She puts the newspaper on the buffet; hands the
letter to* JOHN.]

MARY: A letter on college stationery. John Bridgman, Esq., M.A.

JOHN [*taking letter*]: Probably about a book I forgot to return to the library twelve years ago!

MARY [*anxiously*]: Did you write about a lecture-
ship?

JOHN [*opens the letter*]: It's Bill Campbell. [*His
face drops, as he reads.*] There's to be a class reunion in
November.

MARY: Bill! Remember the times we had?

JOHN: He hopes you and the children are well. He's
still a bachelor—just waiting till I kick off.

MARY [*with a little laugh*]: Why, he wouldn't look
twice at me now!

JOHN: He'll be at the reunion, as Class Secretary.
Will I be there, as President? And what am I doing with
myself now? [*Tossing the letter aside.*] That's the sim-
plest question to answer, and the most difficult!

OTHER SELF: Class President, most likely to succeed,
member of the athletic council, crack runner—class failure, with one solid distinction, a *breakdown!*

MARY: You should go. Will it cost much?

JOHN: They suggest one hundred dollars towards a
new swimming pool. I'll send a note—with regrets.

OTHER SELF: Mary ought to marry Bill. He could
give her everything. You're holding up their lives. Why
don't you just slip out?

MARY: You never wrote to him about a job?

JOHN: How could I, Mary? You know how we were,
the three of us?

MARY: That was years ago. I'm just a college memo-
ry, and if he saw me now—

OTHER SELF: He'd say she was as lovely as ever.

MARY: Well, twelve years are twelve years—and college is a long way back.

JOHN: You could have married Bill.

MARY: I don't go to the highest bidder! I married the

man I loved—it's as simple as that! Don't you *want* to understand?

JOHN: It must take courage to be a woman, gambling your entire life on—

MARY: Yes, it does take a lot of courage! And it takes a lot of courage for a man to justify a woman's faith, too! Why do you allow one upset to shake you so?

JOHN: You've never had to fight shadows.

MARY: Perhaps you won too easily, too often. You weren't toughened to face failure!

JOHN [*flaring up*]: Is anyone?

MARY: Yes! My father, for instance.

JOHN [*with a trace of sarcasm*]: The late and great businessman?

MARY: Mother remembers! In 1932, he was out of work for eleven months. Finally, he got a job at twenty a week, from a total stranger. He pocketed his pride because he wouldn't accept failure. If your friends won't help you, try strangers! Begin again! Like my father. If you're the man I married, you would—

OTHER SELF: But *are* you the man she married?

JOHN [*shoving his chair back*]: I guess I'd—better start downtown.

MARY: Feeling sorry for yourself won't get you around the corner! [*Thrusting the newspaper at him.*] See if there's anything new. [*The doorbell rings.*] One of these days—

> [*She goes to answer the door.* JOHN *opens the newspaper, scans the employment section.*]

OTHER SELF [*peering over* JOHN's *shoulder*]: "Man to sell new invention. Carpenters wanted. Electronics engineers. Clerks for supermarket. Auditor—*quality references.*" [JOHN *slams the paper down.*] Why'd you leave your last job? Men don't leave firms like Bainard and Company without a good reason. There's the big question mark! And the Rest Home. How do you know you're cured? A mental disease can flare up again, like a cannon-cracker. *Can* you assume any responsibility? Will anyone give you the opportunity now? Aren't you wasting your time? Wouldn't there be more pride and satisfaction in death?

MARY [*returning*]: It wasn't anything.

JOHN: Nothing?

MARY: Just a man looking for some work to do.

JOHN [*sinking back into his chair*]: Yes, it was nothing. Poor devil!

MARY: I'm sorry, John. I didn't mean that. Is there anything in the paper?

JOHN: For others, perhaps.

MARY [*clearing the dishes*]: You'll remember to drop in at Mother's?

JOHN: Sure, on the way home.

MARY: Just pick up the parcels and pay no attention to what she ways.

JOHN: I won't get involved in any conversation; don't worry.

MARY: I'll just wash these up. I'm due at Jenny Marven's at about ten.

JOHN [*looking up*]: I thought you couldn't stand her?

MARY: I can't, but she's a clever woman. [*She takes the dishes into the kitchen.*]

OTHER SELF: Yes, keep in with Mother! That wise old woman didn't believe in you from the first! Once you're out of the way, Mary and the girls could live in that big house, shaded from the world by large elms and willows.

[*The telephone rings.* JOHN *rises, crosses to phone.*]

JOHN: Hello? Oh, yes, Mrs. Marven? Yes, I'll ask her. [*He puts the phone down; calls to* MARY.] Mary? Mrs. Marven would like to know if you could come to your typing lesson this afternoon instead of this morning?

[MARY *dashes in rather nervously.*]

MARY: I'll speak to her. [*She picks up the phone.*] Yes, Jenny? Of course. Quite all right; you needn't apologize. I could make it at two. 'Bye. [*She hangs up and is about to return to the kitchen.*]

JOHN [*stopping her*]: So you're taking typing?

MARY: Yes, Jenny's an excellent teacher.

JOHN: Secretaries make respectable salaries these days.

MARY: Yes, very good.

JOHN: Enough to keep a husband till he gets a job!

MARY: Oh, John, I—I didn't want you to know! I just thought—well, lots of women work. I can stifle my pride; why can't you? And when you're working again, I'll remain home.

OTHER SELF: And—when you're dead—

JOHN [*pause*]: It was very sensible, Mary. I'm— glad you did this.

MARY: You're not angry, John?

JOHN: I just told you, I thought it was very sensible! How much gas is there in the car?

MARY: The tank was half full yesterday. There's a five-dollar bill in the cash envelope, if you need more. [*She returns to the kitchen.*]

JOHN [*significantly*]: No, a half-tank's enough.

OTHER SELF: Yes, that ought to do it. The garage is well-built. Lock the doors, and just get the motor running.

JOHN [*quietly*]:

> Go to the dreamless bed
> Where grief reposes;
> The book of toil is read;
> The long day closes.

OTHER SELF: The reunion will pause for a moment, in silence. Ed Murkel will send a large wreath, scented with Scotch. The doctors and the nurses in the long white corridors will nod their heads. The girls will continue to grow, thanks to that new cereal. And Mary will weep for a short time. Good luck, Bill!

JOHN [*wretchedly*]: *Pride!* What else have I left? [*He ambles over to the window, peers out. Suddenly, a look of frustration darkens his face. Shouting.*] Mary! [*A second later, MARY rushes in.*]

MARY [*apprehensively*]: What is it? You're feeling all right?

JOHN [*pointing out the window*]: The car. Look!

MARY [*without looking*]: Yes, it's in the yard.

JOHN: But I put it in the garage last night. I remember, I—I'm sure.

MARY: I know, dear. I took it out.

JOHN: Why?

MARY: The people next door have a new car. They offered me twenty dollars a month for our garage.

JOHN [*numbly*]: I see.

MARY: It won't hurt our old car—standing out there —and it isn't getting much use now.

JOHN [*wheeling on her*]: Why don't you sell it, then? You seem to be a better manager than I am!

MARY: John! [*Pause.*] One day we'll look back on all this and laugh. [*Folding table cloth.*] Look at the Cranes. They've got three cars, yet they're drifting apart. We've only one, but we're coming closer together.

JOHN: Yes, we're learning about each other, aren't we? I'd no idea you were a business woman.

MARY: I'm just trying to do what I can.

JOHN [*gazing out the window and speaking almost to himself*]: I wonder what scrap's worth today?

OTHER SELF: Human scrap—nothing. Now, a car is different. What a poor creature you are! Can't even die when you want to.

MARY [*stopping*]: I'm sorry, John. I'll consult you next time about renting.

JOHN: Never mind. You're twenty dollars a month richer. It just gave me a turn, seeing it out in the yard.

MARY [*compassionately*]: Life is cluttered with odd turns.

[*She goes into the kitchen with the cloth. After she disappears,* JOHN *crosses to the buffet, quietly removes a small, dark bottle from one of the drawers.*]

OTHER SELF [*as* JOHN *unscrews the bottle cap*]: What did Dr. Menzies say? "Five on the tongue of a man will kill an ass." That was to make you careful. We'll be careful—very careful. We'll take *six*.

[*JOHN turns the bottle upside down in the palm of*

his hand; two pills drop out. He shakes the bottle
more vigorously, desperately. MARY *returns.*]

MARY [*calmly*]: I wish you wouldn't take those,
John. You know how strong they are.

JOHN [*bewildered*]: But—there were about a dozen?

MARY: Let me have that bottle.

JOHN: I—thought it might be a big day. I've lots to
do.

MARY [*as he reluctantly hands her the bottle*]: I
spoke to Dr. Menzies. He wanted you to ease off these
things.

JOHN [*lost*]: Ease off?

MARY: So, every day, I've destroyed one. You see,
John, you haven't missed them.

JOHN [*beaten*]: No, not until now.

MARY [*pocketing the bottle and changing the
subject*]: I was going to order some ice cream for the
children's supper. Perhaps you could get it? And three
packages of soap flakes.

JOHN [*restraining the sarcasm*]: I'll do that—and
the parcels from Mother.

OTHER SELF: Little errands to keep your mind off
yourself, make you think you're of some use. Just like a
kid.

MARY: I saw an ad in the paper yesterday. A judge
wants someone to look after his estate. That might be
interesting.

JOHN: Sure, for a single man.

MARY: They'd consider a couple. I wouldn't mind a
year in the country.

JOHN: And the girls?

MARY: Mother would be glad to look after them.

JOHN: I won't have her sneering at me to the girls!
No! We'll keep our home going till the money's gone.
Then, you can go to your mother's.

OTHER SELF: There are things worse than death. Life
at Mother's, for example. At least, you can choose your
hell.

MARY: Very well. We won't discuss it, but she did say her home could be ours, any time.

JOHN: With reservations about her poor, incapable, son-in-law, no doubt!

MARY: Oh, John, You know Mother means well.

JOHN: So do I!

[*He sinks into the chair, thrusts open the newspaper, anxious to conlude the discussion.*]

MARY [*with a shrug*]: Well, there's always work for a good secretary.

JOHN [*suddenly; bolting upright*]: Did you see this?

MARY: I haven't had a chance to look at the morning paper.

JOHN: Harper's dead!

MARY [*stops*]: When?

JOHN: The funeral's this afternoon.

MARY [*a thought*]: Do you think they'll want you back?

JOHN: After being tossed out like a thieving office boy? They'd have to crawl first.

MARY: There must be something they haven't explained. Perhaps they couldn't. Why don't you call Bainard? You still know the business.

JOHN: Do I? Do I know anything—anymore?

MARY: Of course you do! Where's your self-confidence?

JOHN: The books were right. That's the only thing I'm sure of. I took off the trial balance myself two days before.

MARY: The market's supposed to be pretty active now.

JOHN [*pause*]: I—didn't tell you this, Mary. Peters and Isard almost took me on, but they didn't like the medical report.

OTHER SELF: Yes, where were you last year? A Rest Home for your nerves? "Nerves" are often mistaken for insanity, and you must have nerves of steel and mental stability in the brokerage business.

MARY: Do whatever you think's right, then. I merely try to make a suggestion.

JOHN [*returning to the newspaper*]: Harper didn't have his job long, did he?

OTHER SELF: Lucky Harper—no more worries—no more fear.

MARY [*fussing about the room*]: If only you'd call Bainard!

JOHN: What's the use, Mary? I don't think I could.

OTHER SELF: How much lower can you go? Surely, your pride's all eaten away by now—at least, the little you thought you had left. But does Mary care?

[*The doorbell rings.*]

JOHN: Shall I get it?

MARY: Yes, will you?

[JOHN *rises, goes to answer the door. A second or two later,* JOHN *returns with* MR. BAINARD, *a conservatively dressed broker of about fifty-five.*]

MARY [*looking up; greatly surprised*]: Mr. Bainard!

BAINARD: Good morning, Mrs. Bridgman. I—telephoned yesterday. When you didn't return my call, John—

MARY: Oh, was it you?

BAINARD: I believe I spoke to your younger daughter.

MARY: She's not very adept at taking telephone messages.

BAINARD: I thought I'd stop by, personally, John, before Harper's funeral.

JOHN: I—was sorry to hear about Harper.

OTHER SELF: You should be the last to be sorry.

MARY: It was quite a shock.

BAINARD [*uncomfortably*]: May I sit down?

MARY: Oh, do, please.

BAINARD [*sits*]: Ever know I was a fool, John?

JOHN [*half smiling*]: Not until you fired me. Then, I didn't understand.

BAINARD [*a long pause*]: This isn't an easy task for me, John.

MARY: Things haven't been "easy" for us, either, Mr. Bainard.

JOHN [*aware of* BAINARD'S *uneasiness*]: What is it? Apparently, this concerns me.

BAINARD: Yes. I'll be frank.

OTHER SELF: Is there frankness left in the world?

BAINARD: Shortly before Harper died, he admitted something to me—and made me swear to get in touch with you.

JOHN: Why?

BAINARD: A little more than a year ago, he stole some bonds.

JOHN: What has that got to do with me?

BAINARD: He made it appear as though you had appropriated them.

JOHN: Harper?

BAINARD: Yes.

JOHN [angrily]: Why wasn't I told before this?

BAINARD: Naturally, until the last, I had full confidence in Harper's sincerity. Then—your breakdown, which more or less substantiated it for me.

MARY: You thought John would steal?

BAINARD: Strange things can happen, even with loyal employees, Mrs. Bridgman.

JOHN: I could have proven my innocence! Why didn't you prosecute me?

BAINARD: You don't prosecute an . . . [He stops short.]

JOHN [bitterly]: An insane man! Go ahead and say it!

BAINARD: I know now, John. There are all types of breakdowns, and there are all types of men.

JOHN [after a moment]: So Harper, in death, is trying to indemnify me.

BAINARD: Things caught up with him. His last moments weren't pleasant.

JOHN: And what about the past year for me?

BAINARD [rising]: I want to make up for that. I hope you'll forgive me, John, and return to the company. [Pause.] Well?

JOHN [indecisively]: I—don't know.

BAINARD: I wish you'd persuade him, Mrs. Bridgman.

MARY [fighting back the tears]: It's for John to de-

cide. He's capable of his *own* decisions, Mr. Bainard.
[JOHN *turns to* MARY. *A sudden awareness, a confidence begins to seep through.*]

BAINARD: My partner and I would like to meet with you at eleven. At the office. You can decide then.

JOHN: I'm—not sure I can make it at eleven. [MARY *turns to him.*] You see, I am not interested in retrogression. The present's all that matters now.

[MARY, *proud of this new awareness in* JOHN, *tenderly takes hold of his arm.*]

BAINARD: This won't be retrogression, I assure you! [*Pause.*] Well, you're in the driver's seat now, John. It's up to you. [*Starts, turns back.*] Oh, disregard that newspaper obituary! Harper took an overdose of sleeping tablets. We're trying to keep it quiet. [*He proceeds to the door.*]

JOHN: Bainard! [BAINARD *stops and turns. Decisively.*] I'll make it, at eleven! [*With this declaration,* JOHN'S OTHER SELF *vanishes, in defeat.*]

BAINARD [*after a second*]: Thank you, John. You've eased my conscience.

[*He goes out; followed by* JOHN. MARY *flutters excitedly about the room. Anxiously, she lifts the lid of the window seat.*]

MARY [*joyously mumbling to herself*]: His briefcase —and his pen! He must have a new suit—there's five dollars for expenses—and— [*Suddenly, her eyes light on the telephone. She rushes over to it and hastily dials.*] Jenny? I—I won't be able to make it this afternoon. My plans are indefinite. Yes, I know—but the fact is, I don't think I have further need of the typing lessons. [*She hangs up quickly, as* JOHN *comes back into the room.*]

JOHN: Did you hear that, Mary? I eased *his* conscience!

MARY: Yes, yes, I heard! Oh, darling!

JOHN [*incredulously*]: Harper taking sleeping pills!

MARY: *He* hadn't the courage to live.

JOHN [*pause*]: Mary, I don't hear the voice any more!

MARY [*stops*]: Which voice?

JOHN: The other part of me; the part that became lost.

MARY [*with finality*]: No, no, that voice is stilled.

JOHN: Perhaps it was a dream; a horrible dream?

MARY: Yes, and you mustn't think of it any more! You've got to get to the office! Didn't I tell you something nice would happen on our anniversary?

JOHN: Don't tell the children until I get home.

MARY: I'll try not to.

JOHN [*a new attitude*]: They really did stick by their old man, didn't they? [*Pause.*] Mary—did *you* ever lose faith?

MARY: Did you?

JOHN [*evading the question*]: Where's my briefcase?

MARY [*crosses to window seat and removes briefcase*]: I've taken excellent care of it!

JOHN [*after a long pause and with his gaze fixed on her*]: Thanks, Mary.

MARY: That's evidence I never lost faith! [*Quickly, concealing her emotions.*] You'd better get a haircut and a shine on the way. I'll make an appointment for you with the tailor.

JOHN: Better wait till the end of the month. [*He starts for the door; then stops, turns back, questioningly.*] It isn't a dream, it is, Mary? Bainard really was here?

MARY [*gently*]: Of course he was!

JOHN: I've been deceived before in dreams.

MARY: You're awake now, John, very much awake. Now, off to the office!

JOHN [*smiling a little*]: Oh! You can't be sending me off like this.

MARY [*worried again*]: What is it?

JOHN [*lightly*]: When did you ever allow me to go to the office without a clean handkerchief?

MARY [*relieved*]: You can have a dozen! [*She hurries to buffet for a handkerchief.*] There, now you're ready for anything!

[*The cloudiness of the day gives way to the sun; the lights begin to brighten.*]

JOHN: Remember that first day I began at Bainard's? [*He begins to laugh.*]

MARY: I gave you so many hankies you bulged!

JOHN [*picks up briefcase*]: 'Bye, darling! [*He kisses her.*]

MARY [*calling after him, as he starts*]: Got your— handkerchief, dear?

JOHN [*calling back*]: Everything I need!

[*He chuckles, as he disappears.* MARY *stands for a moment as though she hardly is able to believe what has happened.*]

MARY: He laughed! God! He really laughed!

[*Unable to control her emotions any longer, she bursts into tears, tears of relief, joy, and of all the anguish of the year gone by.*]

[*Curtain.*]

BIOGRAPHICAL NOTES

STEPHEN LEACOCK. When he was six years old Stephen Leacock (1869–1944) came to Canada with his parents on an emigrant ship that was equipped with sails to help out the steam engine; before his long life ended, he had included among his many writing tasks a promotional piece for Pan American Airways. Few modern writers have been busier or more versatile. As a professor of Economics and Political Science at McGill University for more than thirty years, he was the author of several learned books related to his profession. His wide-ranging interests led him also to write two highly regarded literary biographies of Mark Twain and Charles Dickens. But the world knows him best as a humorist. Among the most popular of his dozens of humorous books are *Literary Lapses* (1910), *Nonsense Novels* (1911), and *Sunshine Sketches* (1912). Many famous comedians have admired Leacock, Charlie Chaplin among them, and have used his comic techniques. In fact, it is easy to imagine the young Chaplin taking the male role in *The Raft*.

ARTHUR HAILEY. The writing career of Arthur Hailey (1920–   ) began during a night flight from Vancouver to Toronto in 1955 when he fell to wondering what would happen if both pilots became sick. Before the plane landed in Toronto, he had worked out the plot of *Flight into Danger*. After ten days of writing he sent the completed script to the Canadian Broadcasting Corporation. The CBC bought it and broadcast it on

April 3, 1956. A new production of the drama was presented in the United States by NBC, and a few months later in England the BBC broadcast the original Canadian version. In November 1957 Paramount released a movie version under the title *Zero Hour*. Revised as a novel, it has been translated into eleven languages and been published in fifteen countries. Finally it was adapted for performance on the live stage. The titles that follow are a mere sampling of this popular author's other writings; chances are that you will recognize some of them: *The Young Doctors* (originally a TV drama, rewritten as a novel in 1959 and finally released as a movie in 1961), *Hotel* (1965), *Airport* (1968), *Wheels* (1971) and *The Moneychangers* (1975).

GEORGE RYGA.   When he was a high-school student in Alberta, George Ryga (1932–   ) was persuaded by his English teacher to submit some samples of his writing in a scholarship competition held by the Banff School of Fine Arts. It was while he was a scholarship student at this summer school that his interest in drama was sparked. By the 1960s he was writing radio scripts to order for the Canadian Broadcasting Corporation. One such script, a brief drama called *Pine-Tree Ghetto,* he tailored to fit into a seven-minute slot on the CBC's *Farm Show*. Since he was becoming interested in television drama about this time, Ryga rewrote the seven-minute radio script into a half-hour TV play and called it *Indian*. It was accepted by the CBC and broadcast in November, 1962. In 1964 Ryga expressed his continuing concern for Canadian Indians in a full length stage-play, *The Ecstasy of Rita Joe*. Overnight the play established his reputation as a leading Canadian dramatist. Since then other plays have followed: *Grass and Wild Strawberries* (1967), *Captives of the Faceless Drummer* (1971), *Sunrise for Sarah* (1973), and *Portrait of Angelica* (1973). His latest play, *Paracelsus,* was planned for performance in Toronto.

ROBERTSON DAVIES. Although he received his early education in Ontario, Robertson Davies (1913–   ) gained his professional stage experience in England, first as an actor and stage manager with the Old Vic Repertory Company, then as a teacher of acting in the Old Vic School. Later he returned to Canada and, until his appointment in 1961 as Master of Massey College in the University of Toronto, was editor and publisher of the *Peterborough Examiner*. Among his plays are *Eros at Breakfast and Other Plays* (1949), *Fortune My Foe* (1949), *At My Heart's Core* (1950), *A Jig for the Gypsy* (1954), and *Hunting Stuart* (1955). He has published five novels: *Tempest Tost* (1951), *Leaven of Malice* (1954), *A Mixture of Frailties* (1958), *Fifth Business* (1970), and *The Manticore* (1972). *Overlaid* is an early comedy (1948), but one that has proved extremely popular. It has been staged countless times and has been broadcast by the CBC twice, first as a radio play and later as a television production.

NORMAN WILLIAMS. Even in high school Norman Williams (1923–   ) was carrying off prizes for creative writing. In the 1950s he turned his talent to account by writing short plays for radio and stage. For three consecutive years he won the Ottawa Little Theatre's Canadian Playwriting Competition (1953, '54, '55). In 1956 six of his prize-winning plays were published under the title *Worlds Apart*. In 1957 his first full-length play, *To Ride a Tiger*, took the Lieutenant Governor's Award in the Dominion Drama Festival. Among his more recent dramas are *He Didn't Even Say Goodbye*, *Take to the Trees*, and *Don't Touch That Phone*, all published in 1972. His authentic portrayal of character and conflict in *Protest* makes it easy to understand why he is so highly regarded a dramatist.

GWEN PHARIS RINGWOOD.   Because she is well known as a playwright with a deep understanding of the human heart, Gwen Pharis Ringwood (1910–   ) is often asked to adjudicate in drama festivals. *Lament for Harmonica*, which won first prize in the 1958 Ottawa Little Theatre's Playwriting Competition, is a good illustration of her gift for revealing character in a few lines of dialogue. Among her widely admired short plays are *Still Stands the House* (1938), *Dark Harvest* (1945), *Widger* (1950), *Stampede* (1956), and *The Deep Has Many Voices* (1966). She has also written librettos for two musicals: *Look Behind You, Neighbour* (1961) and *The Road Runs North* (1968). She has published one novel, *Younger Brother* (1959), and is now working on another, to be entitled *You Walk a Narrow Bridge*. Her plays and stories are usually set in the Canadian West, where she has lived most of her life.

GEORGE BOWERING.   An Assistant Professor of English at Simon Fraser University, George Bowering (1935–   ) is best known as a poet. Since the early 1960s collections of his poems have appeared each year: *Sticks and Stones* (1963), *Points on the Grid* (1964), *The Man in Yellow Boots* (1965), *The Silver Wire* (1966), *Baseball* (1967), *Two Police Poems* (1968), *Rocky Mountain Foot* (1969), *Sitting in Mexico* (1970), *Touch: Selected Poems* (1971), and *Autobiology* (1972). He has also written a novel, *Mirror on the Floor* (1967), and some short plays for television. *The Home for Heroes*, the television play chosen for this book, treats comically a problem common in Bowering's other writing: In this frightening technological age, how can an ordinary man find out who he really is?

MERRILL DENISON. Until *Brothers in Arms* was performed in the University of Toronto's Hart House Theatre in 1921, it was customary for Canadian writers to depict rural characters as possessing a moral and physical superiority gained through their close contact with the soil. The reader will note just how far the backwoodsmen in *Brothers in Arms* fall short of this idea. Several other of Denison's short plays satirizing this notion of rural superiority were published in a collection entitled *The Unheroic North* (1923). A later work of fiction, *Boobs in the Woods* (1927), showed the same satirical intent. More recently Merrill Denison (1893–) has concentrated on writing industrial histories. Among these latter works are *The Power to Go: The History of the Automotive Industry in America* (1956), *The People's Power, the History of Ontario's Hydro* (1960), and *Canada's First Bank: A History of the Bank of Montreal* (1967).

KAY HILL. ·Before she became a full-time writer in 1957, Kay Hill (1917–) was a secretary and court reporter in Halifax, Nova Scotia. The careful listening demanded by both those jobs may account for the marvellous ear for East Coast dialogue that she demonstrates in *Cobbler Stick to Thy Last*. That play, which represents her in this collection, has been produced by one stage company fifty times. Although her short stage plays are popular, she writes most of her dramatic scripts for radio and television. She has lost count of those prepared for radio, and estimates that by 1970 she had written about twenty-five plays for TV. Two collections of her short stories are well known to younger readers: *Glooskap and His Magic* (1963) and *More Glooskap Stories* (1970). At the present time she is continuing her research into early Nova Scotian history, particularly the fur trade, in preparation for a forthcoming book.

WILFRID WERRY.   For twelve years Wilfrid Werry
(1897–   ) lectured on various aspects of the craft of
writing at Sir George Williams University in Montreal.
Proving that he is an able practitioner of what he teach-
es, he is also the author of several interesting plays. In
addition to *Breakdown* he has written *The Bag of Earth*,
which was staged by the Ottawa Little Theatre, and a
full-length work, *Not Without Right*, a drama set in
Elizabethan times with Shakespeare as its main character. This play won a Special Interest mention in the
1959 Stratford Globe and Mail Playwriting Competition. He is also a B.Com. and M.A. from McGill and a
Chartered Accountant. After lecturing in English and
Accounting at The Montreal Institute of Technology he
became Acting Director. At the present time he is writing in the Canary Islands—particularly articles, plays,
and murder stories.